D1444473

THE

ORIGINS OF

POPULAR SUPERSTITIONS

AND CUSTOMS

The Origins of Popular Superstitions and Customs

BY

T. SHARPER KNOWLSON

Author of

" The Art of Thinking," etc.

LONDON

T. WERNER LAURIE LTD.

COBHAM HOUSE, 24 & 26 WATER LANE, E.C.4

1910

REPUBLISHED BY GALE RESEARCH COMPANY, BOOK TOWER, DETROIT, 1968

Library of Congress Catalog Card
Number 68–30946

PREFACE.

THE following pages are based on Brand's *Popular Antiquities*, the edition published in 1841, supplemented by the results of later investigation. My aim has been to deal only with those superstitions and customs which are operative at the present time ; and, so far as is possible, to trace these to their original sources. In some cases the task is fairly easy, in others very difficult ; whilst in a few instances the " prime origin," to use the words of Brand, is absolutely unattainable. Still, in these days of pageantry, when the British people show some signs of periodically reviewing the picturesque life of bygone times, it will be a source of satisfaction if in this book I succeed in tracing, though it be for a century or two, the thoughts and habits which were born in a remote past.

CONTENTS.

SECTION II.   Marriage Superstitions and Customs

SECTION III.   Divination and Omens

SECTION IV. Miscellaneous Superstitions and Customs

I
The Origins of Popular Superstitions and Customs

INTRODUCTION.

THE true origin of superstition is to be found in early man's effort to explain Nature and his own existence; in the desire to propitiate Fate and invite Fortune; in the wish to avoid evils he could not understand; and in the unavoidable attempt to pry into the future. From these sources alone must have sprung that system of crude notions and practices still obtaining among savage nations; and although in more advanced nations the crude system gave place to attractive mythology, the moving power was still the same; man's interpretation of the world was equal to his ability to understand its mysteries— no more, no less. For this reason the superstitions which, to use a Darwinian word, *persist*, are of special interest, as showing a psychological habit of some importance. Of this, more anon.

The first note in all superstitions is that of *ignorance.* Take three representative and widely different cases. The first is a Chinaman living about one thousand years before Christ. He has before him the "Book of Changes," and is about to divine the future by geometrical figures; the second is a Roman lady, bent on the same object, but using the shapes of molten wax dropped into water ; the third is a Stock Exchange speculator seated before a modern clairvoyant in Bond Street, earnestly seeking light on the future of his big deal in Brighton A. The operating cause here is a desire to know the future, and, so long as man is man, so long will he either rely on the divinations of the past, or invent new ones more in keeping with mental science. But ignorance exists in several varieties, and one of them has to do, not with the future, but with the well-established present ; in other words, an accepted doctrine may be based on a misinterpretation of the facts. As Trenchard remarks in his *Natural History of Superstition*, " Man's curiosity is in excess of his capacity to interpret Nature and life." Thus early man attributed a living spirit to everything—to his fellows, to the lower animals, to the trees, the mountains, and the rivers. Probably these conclusions were as good as his intelligence would allow, but they became the mental stock-in-trade of all races, and were handed down from one generation to another, constituting a barrier to be broken down before newer and truer ideas of life could prevail. And the same contention applies equally to the superstition of the moment. The woman who will not pay a call unless she wears a particular amulet, or the man who starts up from a table of thirteen, his face blanched and his blood cold, are just as truly, though not in the same degree, the victims of ignorance as the animist who tried to propitiate the anger of the spirit of the stream. Ignorance is the atmosphere in which alone such superstitions can live.

Allied with ignorance is *fear*, which is the second element calling for notice. Fear, too, has its varieties, some of them both natural and justifiable. If I visit an electrical power - house and know nothing of its machinery and appointments, I am very chary what I touch and prefer to keep my hands to myself lest I make a mistake. Rational fear, however, is the offspring of a reasoned knowledge of danger. It is *irrational* fear which forms the bogey of superstition. The misfortune of early man was to have experiences more numerous and subtle than he could understand ; to his power of analysis they were altogether unyielding ; and yet his unrestrained imagination demanded a working theory of some kind, and he got one, grounded in ignorance and fear. An earthquake is a phenomenon calculated to strike terror into the heart of all but the strongest man ; no wonder then that the primitive mind invented all sorts of ideas about spirits of the under world, and ascribed to gloomy caverns the possession of dragons and other fearsome enemies of the race. The thunder, the lightning and the tempest ; the blight which spoiled the sources of food ; the sudden attack of mysterious sickness, and a hundred other fatalities were to him more than merely natural forces busily employed in working out their natural destiny ; they were Powers to be propitiated. That is the third note of the superstitious mind ; its effort to propitiate intelligent and semi-intelligent forces by suitable beliefs, rites, ceremonies, and penances. Where ignorance and fear beget a sense of danger, knowledge, even defective knowledge, is always equal to the task of inventing a way of escape.

But if these be the prime origins of superstition, what are the secondary origins? If "the belief in the existence and proximity of a world of spirits, and a fear of such spirits, is the only solution of all the curious religions, customs, ceremonies, and superstitions of pagan life,"[1] what are the other causes which modified these primitive guesses at the riddle of existence? The answer is twofold: (1) The old causes have never ceased to be operative, though the manner of expression has changed; and (2) The new causes were the advent of world religions, of social transformations, and of political separation.

As an illustration of the old causes in a new application, I will take ignorance once more. Lord Mahon, in his *History of England*, tells us: "It chanced that six children in one family died in quick succession of a sudden and mysterious illness—their feet having mortified and dropped off. Professor Henslow, who resides at no great distance from Wattisham, has given much attention to the records of this case, and has made it clear in his excellent essay on the *Diseases of Wheat*, that in all probability their death was owing to the improvident use of deleterious food —the ergot of rye. But he adds that in the neighbourhood the popular belief was firm that these poor children had been the victims of sorcery and witchcraft."[2] This was little over forty years ago in "Christian England." Four hundred years ago, or twice or thrice that number, it was just the same— the domination of ignorance.

But the causes called secondary offer a new field of

1 Dorman: *Origin of Superstition*, p. 385.
2 *The Gentleman's Magazine* (1857).

enquiry. Take the advent of Christianity with its point of view diametrically opposed to the religions of the period. What was the effect on paganism? It was seen in the Christianising of many of the old superstitions and customs, and in the creation of a group of new ones. To the student of origins there is no fact more significent than this, and none to which he can look forward more hopefully for intelligent explanations of prevalent beliefs and practices. He is on historic ground, and whereas "most of those who have endeavoured to account for the various superstitions of savage races have done so by crediting them with a much more elaborate system of ideas than they in reality possess,"[1] he can give chapter and verse for the modifications and developments in the first century of the Christian era. Sir Isaac Newton was not a historian, but he was right when he said (in his book on *Prophesies*) that "the Heathens were delighted with the Festivals of their Gods, and unwilling to part with those ceremonies; therefore Gregory, Bishop of Neo-Cæsarea in Pontus, to facilitate their conversion, instituted annual Festivals to the Saints and Martyrs; hence the keeping of Christmas with ivy, feasting, plays, and sports, came in the room of Bacchanalia and Saturnalia; the celebrating May Day with flowers, in the room of the Floralia; and the Festivals to the Virgin Mary, *John the Baptist*, and divers of the Apostles, in the room of the solemnities at the entrance of the Sun into the Signs of the Zodiac in the old Julian Calendar."

But the *events* of Christianity, the birth, life, and

[1] *Avebury, Origin of Civilisation. p. 213*   B

death of Christ, were themselves the basis of new superstitions. For example, the notion that to sit down at a table of a Christian is unlucky, can have no other origin than that of the Last Supper, and all Good Friday superstitions are of course Christian, that is, although discountenanced by the Church they are based upon Christian history.

With the Reformation came a radical force that tended to push all the old superstitions and customs into oblivion. The analogy between the pagan and Christian forms was detected and enlarged upon with the utmost severity of condemnation. Randolph's *Poems* (1646) tells us something of the spirit of these Puritan criticisms :—

> "These teach that dancing is a Jezabel,
> And Barley-Break the ready way to Hell;
> The Morice Idols, Whitsun Ales can be
> But profane reliques of a Jubilee:
> There is a zeal t' expresse how much they do
> The Organs hate, have silenc'd Bagpipes too;
> And harmless May-Poles all are rail'd upon,
> As if they were the Tow'rs of Babylon."

Ultimately the *custom* was attacked before the superstition in the hope that the decay of the one would result in the disappearance of the other. Such hopes were not altogether disappointed, but as is evident from the crowd of superstitions that did not die, or have since been revived, the modifying effect of Puritanism cannot be said to have done more than create a prejudice against the rites and associations of the Catholic Church. But that Church has always been the fountain of superstition, for when Newman declared his belief that all the wood in Continental Churches, alleged to have been part of the Cross (although enough to timber an ironclad), was *really* what it professed to be—probably miraculously multiplied by Divine force like the loaves and fishes—we can see a little better the Puritan's point of view. The eye of the Papist was ever on the look out for signs and portents of grace in the realm of Nature and material things. A good instance of this is found in the old notion of the shaking aspen. Christ is alleged to have been crucified on aspen wood, and from that time the boughs of aspen trees "have been filled with horror and trembled ceaselessly." Unfortunately for the probability of this story, the shivering of the aspen in the breeze may be traced to other than a supernatural cause. The construction of its foliage is particularly adapted for motion: a broad leaf is placed upon a long footstalk, so flexible as scarcely to be able to support the leaf in an upright posture; the upper part of this stalk, on which the play or action seems mainly to depend, is contrary to the nature of footstalks in general, being perfectly flattened, and as an eminent botanist has acutely observed, is placed at a right angle with the leaf, being thus particularly fitted to receive the impulse of every wind that blows. The stalk is furnished with three strong nerves, placed parallel and acting in unison with each other; but towards the base the stalk becomes round, and then the nerves assume a triangular form, and constitute three distinct supports and counteractions to each other's motions."

This disposition to see a religious message in everything secular is responsible for a good many local superstitions. "All things praise Thee," was taken in its literal sense.

An example, which in these days would be considered ludicrous, of the manner in which our ancestors made external nature bear witness to our Lord, occurs in what is called the Prior's Chamber, in the small Augustinian house of Shubbrede, in the parish of Linchmere in Sussex. On the wall is a fresco of the Nativity; and certain animals are made to give their testimony to that event in words which somewhat resemble, or may be supposed to resemble, their natural sounds. A cock, in the act of crowing, stands at the top, and a label, issuing from his mouth, bears the words, *Christus natus est.* A duck inquires, *Quando, quando?* A raven answers, *In hâc nocte.* A cow asks, *Ubi, ubi?* And a lamb bleats out, *Bethlehem.*

This devout attitude is by no means absent from the Protestant mind, ancient and modern. Quite logically, too ; for, if there is an active Providence, that Providence must manifest itself in some outward and visible sign. Hence we find to-day what we find throughout history, that there are superstitions fostered by the religious disposition, and others that may be called social—for want of a better term. They are accepted apart from any ecclesiastical creed. The faithful will agree that relics are good to be adored ; the non-religionist has no opinion about relics, but he will carefully avoid walking under a ladder.

Now we come to the most difficult question of all : why is it that some of the superstitions in the past persist in the present ? Why do we, in an age of increasing knowledge, still retain some of our fears —the offspring of ignorance ? We can understand the perpetuation of a custom, even when its inner significance has gone, but a living superstition is a different thing.

One reason must be sought in the fact that superstition has always been *contagious*. This is amusingly set forth by Bagehot in his *Physics and Politics*, although probably India contains more mysteries than he allowed :—

" In *Eothen* there is a capital description of how every sort of European resident in the East—even the shrewd merchant and the 'post-captain with his bright, wakeful eye of command '—comes soon to believe in witchcraft, and to assure you in confidence that 'there is really something in it ;' he has never seen anything convincing himself, but he has seen those who have seen those who have seen those who have seen ; in fact he has lived in an atmosphere of infectious belief, and he has inhaled it."

If this is true now, it must have been more profoundly true in past centuries. The presence everywhere of the same superstition, though in different forms, is a testimony to the power of contagious fears. Children brought up in the atmosphere of credulity do not often rise above it. White in his *Selborne* observes :—" It is the hardest thing in the world to shake off superstitious prejudices ; they are sucked in as it were with our mother's milk ; and, growing up with us at a time when they take the fastest hold and make the most lasting impressions, become so interwoven with our very constitutions, that the strongest sense is required to disengage ourselves from them. No wonder, therefore, that the lower people retain them their whole lives through, since their minds are not in-vigorated by a liberal education, and therefore not enabled to make any efforts adequate to the occasion." He adds that such a preamble seems to be necessary before he enters on the superstitions of his own district, lest he should be suspected of exaggeration in a recital of practices too gross for an enlightened age.

But — and this is a further reason for the persistence which is the object of our enquiry— there is *a superstitious mind*, quite independent of education and training. One has already referred to Newman, who possessed as subtle an intellect as any man in the nineteenth century; there is Dr Johnson, who believed something bad would happen if he did not touch every post as he passed along the road or street; he had for some reason built that idea into his mind, and nothing could dislodge it. Take another instance, this time from a source where one would not expect it. J. D. Rockefeller, reputed to be the world's wealthiest man, is of Puritan or Nonconformist associations, and yet, according to a London journal which specialises in personal items, he pleads guilty to a pet superstition. For years he has carried an eagle stone in his pocket. This is a kind of hollow stone, containing in its cavity some concretions which rattle on shaking the stone. It is of a brownish tint, and is often carried by the eagle to its nest. Superstition ascribes wonderful virtue to these stones when actually found in the bird's nest. They are a charm against disaster, shipwreck, and other calamities. A ribbon passed through the perforation of the stone is said to possess even more virtues than the stone itself, and when

Mr Rockefeller wishes to confer a particular favour upon someone, he gives him a small piece of this ribbon.

But the great reason why superstitions persist is because they are, in part, doctrines about matters concerning which we as yet know little. Mental and occult influences are the staple commodities of most of those practices which modern science condemns as meaningless. Of these influences we are in partial ignorance, and until that ignorance is dissolved we shall always have the crystal gazer and the clairvoyant in our midst, despite the activity of the police. True, some of the remarkable " coincidences " related in solemn tones, amid breathless silence, are receiving their quietus at the hands of the expert in hypnotism and auto-suggestion ; from this standpoint we may eventually be able to justify some of the stories about charms and amulets, as well as to develop a useful moral agency. But in regard to occult powers, especially what is known as black magic, we are still in darkness, mainly because those who are competent to investigate laugh the problems out of court as not worthy of attention. This is a pity, because, if there are any superstitions at all which have an origin that can be tested here and now, it is the group belonging to the occult section, dealing with the things in heaven and earth "not dreamed of in our philosophy." In view of such discoveries as have been made by Lombroso and others, not so much in magic as in mental forces, it would appear very desirable to initiate enquiries into the so-called evil side of man's powers, the persistent tradition of which has come down from remote antiquity, and surrounding which are strange superstitions and nightmare stories. It is because men of all classes have some modified belief in these vicious powers that a kind of half probability is accorded to beliefs of a more innocent hue. To read the narratives of modern travellers in the East, men with no axe to grind, and not suffering from "imagination," is to have one's curiosity awakened to the highest degree; for they tell us of powers to which there is no corresponding agency in the West. If early races in the same territory possessed the same powers, it is easy to understand the tenacity with which they held on to the beliefs in the supernatural as they understood it.

Reviewing the whole subject, without prejudice, it seems to the present writer that the right attitude of mind towards the superstitions that are still operative is not one of mere condemnation, or lofty indifference; it should be one of sympathetic inquiry, for the psychological and scientific data available are of the highest interest; and just as astronomy arose out of astrology and chemistry out of alchemy, so from the occult world we may some day attain developments in mental science, equally distinctive and equally useful in the service of the race.

DAYS AND SEASONS

DAYS AND SEASONS

(1) CANDLEMAS DAY.

As the celebration of the Purification of the Virgin Mary, this day hardly needs the tracing of an origin, but the following from Brand is decidedly interesting:—

"How this candle-bearing on Candlemas Day came first up, the author of our English Festival declareth in this manner: "Somtyme," said he, "when the Romaines by great myght and royal power conquered all the world, they were so proude, that they forgat God, and made them divers gods after their own lust. And so among all they had a god that they called Mars, that had been tofore a notable knight in battayle; and so they prayed to hym for help, and for that they would speed the better of this knight, the people prayed and did great worship to his mother, that was called Februa, after which woman much people have opinion that the moneth February is called. Wherefore the second daie of thys moneth is Candlemass Day. The Romaines this night went about the city of Rome with torches and candles brenning in worship of this woman Februa, for hope to have the more helpe and succoure of her sonne Mars.

"Then there was a Pope that was called Sergius,

and when he saw Christian people drawn to this false maumetry and untrue belief, he thought to undo this foule use and custom, and turn it into God's worship and our Lady's, and gave commandment that all Christian people should come to church and offer up a candle brennyng, in the worship that they did to this woman Februa, and do worship to our Lady and to her sonne our Lord Jesus Christ. So that now this feast is solemnly hallowed thorowe all Christendome. And every Christian man and woman of covenable age is bound to come to church and offer up their candles, as though they were bodily with our Lady, hopying for this reverence and worship, that they do to our Lady, to have a great rewarde in heaven."

In some parts of the country, Scotland particularly, Candlemas has assumed a secular garb by becoming the first of the quarterly terms; and in Cornwall old customs of a slightly different character are kept up. I select from a London morning paper (1910) a few paragraphs relating to an ancient custom.

CANDLEMAS CUSTOM.

COLLECTING A RENT OF BREAD, BEER, BRAWN, AND CHEESE AT GODOLPHIN.

This being Candlemas Day, the old Cornish manor house of Godolphin, now a farm-house, was visited, telegraphs our Penzance correspondent, by the reeve of the manor of Lamburne, who came to collect, with time-honoured ceremony, a rent-charge upon the estate.

In the presence of a crowd of curious neighbours

and sight-seers, the reeve knocked thrice upon the oaken door.

" I come," he cried, "to demand my lord's just dues—eight groats and a penny, a loaf, a cheese, a collar of brawn, and a jack of the best beer in the house. God save the King and the lord of the manor."

When the doors were opened, the reeve and some forty guests sat down to breakfast together.

(2) VALENTINE'S DAY (February 14th).

Although St. Valentine's Day is only observed in a very few places in the United Kingdom, and tends towards a speedy disappearance, it is a custom which, for this reason, is specially worth notice, inasmuch as some of us who are by no means old can remember the days when the sending of " Valentines " by a certain section of society was quite a festival in itself —almost as vigorous as the fashion of 'Xmas cards is at the moment.   St. Valentine was a Christian Bishop, who is alleged to have suffered martyrdom in 271 A.D., on February 14th.   Roman youths and maidens on this day were accustomed to select partners, and the Church, fulfilling its work of re-placing heathen divinities by ecclesiastical saints, allotted the day to St. Valentine.   Butler in his *Lives of the Saints* says :—" To abolish the heathen, lewd, superstitious custom of boys drawing the names of girls, in honour of their goddess Februata Juno, on the 15th of February, several zealous Pastors sub-stituted the names of Saints in billets given on that day.   St. Frances de Sales severely forbad the custom of Valentines, or giving boys in writing the

names of girls to be admired and attended on by
them ; and to abolish it, he changed it into giving
billets with the names of certain Saints, for them to
honour and imitate in a particular manner."

Apparently the effort was not altogether successful,
for the specimen Valentine verses that have come
down to us from old English times, as well as some of
the pictures which used to be flaunted in shop-
windows in the last century, testify to the intimate
connection between the Pagan idea and its attempted
Christian reconstruction. St. Valentine, as a good
man, can have no reason to thank the Church for its
attentions to his name.

Gay has left us a poetical description of some rural
ceremonies used on the morning of this day :

> " Last Valentine, the day when birds of kind,
> Their paramours with mutual chirpings find,
> I early rose, just at the break of day,
> Before the sun had chas'd the stars away ;
> A-field I went, amid the morning dew,
> To milk my kine (for so should house-wives do).
> Thee first I spied, and the first swain we see,
> In spite of Fortune, shall our true love be."

Evidently the women-folk used to take Valentine's
Day somewhat seriously. Witness the following from
an old book—the *Connoisseur* :—" Last Friday was
Valentine Day, and the night before I got five bay-
leaves, and pinned four·of them to the four corners of
my pillow, and the fifth to the middle ; and then, if I
dreamt of my sweetheart, Betty said we should be
married before the year was out. But to make it
more sure I boiled an egg hard, and took out the
yolk and filled it with salt ; and when I went to bed
ate it, shell and all, without speaking or drinking

after it. We also wrote our lovers' names upon bits of paper, and rolled them up in clay, and put them into water : and the first that rose up was to be our Valentine. Would you think it, Mr Blossom was my man. I lay a-bed and shut my eyes all the morning till he came to our house ; for I would not have seen another man before him for all the world."

The dying of St. Valentine's Day is a testimony to the growth of a sense of restraint and fine feeling. But even this year (1910) in London one can see the old vulgar Valentine shown in shop windows.

(3) SIMNEL SUNDAY.

The fourth Sunday in Lent is in most Lancashire towns called Simnel Sunday, and Simnel cakes— ornamental and rich cakes like those made at 'Xmas time—are eaten. A⋅ writer in *The Gentleman's Magazine* (1867) informs us that "from time beyond memory thousands of persons come from all parts to that town (Bury) to eat Simnels. Formerly, nearly every shop was open, with all the public-houses, quite in defiance of the law respecting the closing during 'service'; but of late years, through the improved state of public opinion, the disorderly scenes to which the custom gave rise have been partially amended. Efforts have been made to put a stop to the practice altogether, but in vain." This was forty years ago, and the trade in Bury "Simnels," owing to quick and cheap transit, has practically put an end to the local celebrations. The origin of the word Simnel is in doubt. In Wright's *Vocabularies* it appears thus :— "Hic arlaecopus=symnelle." This form was in use during the fifteenth century. In the *Dictionarius* of

John de Garlande, completed in Paris in the thirteenth century, it appears thus :—" Simeneus = placentae = simnels." Such cakes were stamped with the figure of Christ or of the Virgin. We can ouly conclude that as cakes—witness the shewbread of the Hebrews —have always occupied an important place in early forms of worship, there was a successful effort in the north to localise a Christianised form of celebration ; for the mixture of joviality and religious austerity which characterised Simnel Sunday in past centuries is in keeping with the same display on other occasions in countries further south.

(4) MAUNDAY THURSDAY (OR SHERE THURSDAY).

There seems to be much dispute between antiquarians as to the origin of both " Maunday " and "Shere," and of course the spelling has the usual vagaries. For instance *The British Apollo* (1709) says :—" Maunday is a corruption of the Latin word *Mandatum*, a command. The day is therefore so called, because as on that day our Saviour washed his disciples' feet, to teach them the great duty ot being humble. And therefore he gives them in command to do as he had done, to imitate their Master in all proper instances of condescension and humility."

On the other hand " Maunday Thursday," says a writer in *The Gentleman's Magazine* (1779), "is the poor people's Thursday, from the Fr. *maundier*, to beg. The King's liberality to the poor on that Thursday in Lent [is at] a season when they are supposed to have lived very low. *Maundiant* is at this day in French a beggar." Which are we to believe? The preponderating weight of evidence seems to be in favour of the former.

In reference to "Shere," one authority says it is so called "for that in old Fathers' days the people would that day shere theyr hedes and clippe theyr berdes and pool theyr heedes, and so make them honest agenst Easter Day." But another writer in *The Gentleman's Magazine* (1779) finds a different origin for the word. "Maundy Thursday, called by Collier, *Shier* Thursday, Cotgrave calls by a word of the same sound and import, *Sheere* Thursday. Perhaps, for I can only go upon conjecture, as *sheer* means *purus mundus*, it may allude to the washing of the disciples' feet (John xiii. 5, et seq.), and be tantamount to clean. Please to observe too, that on that day *they also washed the Altars:* so that the term in question may allude to that business."

Here again one feels there is no other course open than to accept the word of the earlier authority. As to the events of the day, I cannot do better than transcribe a section from *The Gentleman's Magazine* for 1731 :—

"Thursday, April 15, beind Maunday Thursday, there was distributed at the Banquetting House, Whitehall, to forty-eight poor men, and forty-eight poor women (the king's age forty-eight) boiled beef and shoulders of mutton, and small bowls of ale, which is called dinner; after that, large wooden platters of fish and loaves, *viz.* undressed, one large old ling, and one large dried cod ; twelve red herrings, and twelve white herrings, and four half quarter loaves. Each person had one platter of this provision ;

after which was distributed to them shoes, stockings, linen and woollen cloth, and leathern bags, with one penny, two penny, three penny, and four penny pieces of silver, and shillings; to each about four pounds in value. His Grace the Lord Archbishop of York, Lord High Almoner, performed the annual ceremony of washing the feet of a certain number of poor in the Royal Chapel, Whitehall, which was formerly done by the kings themselves, in imitation of our Saviour's pattern of humility, etc. James the Second was the last king who performed this in person."

But some Catholic monarchs still persevere in this pious act, even to the washing of beggars' feet. In England, the king's Maundy is given at Westminster Abbey at a specially convened service, and those who receive it are carefully chosen from London parishes.

(5) SHROVE TUESDAY.

Shrove Tuesday, or as we know it to-day, "Pancake Tuesday" seems in the olden times to have been a season of merriment, horseplay, and cruelty, as if the participants were determined to have their fling ere Lent set in with its sombre feelings and proscription of joy. Prostitutes were hounded out of their dwellings with a view to segregation during the Lenten term; "cock-throwing" was indulged in, a cock being tied to a stake and pelted by the onlookers; and all kinds of rough games were played, the women and the men joining in the "fun." The frying and eating of pancakes is apparently the only item left to us of this rather choice list of festivities. Taylor in his *Jack-a-Lent*

(1630) gives the following curious account of the custom :—

"Shrove - Tuesday, at whose entrance in the morning all the whole kingdom is inquiet, but by that time the clocke strikes eleven, which (by the help of a knavish sexton) is commonly before nine, then there is a bell rung, cal'd the Pancake-bell, the sound whereof makes thousands of people distracted, and forgetful either of manners or humanitie; then there is a thing called wheaten floure, which the cookes do mingle with water, eggs, spice, and other tragical, magical inchantments, and then they put it by little and little into a frying pan of boiling suet, where it makes a confused dismal hissing, (like the Lernean Snakes in the reeds of Acheron, Stix, or Phlegeton) until at last, by the skill of the Cooke, it is transformed into the forme of a Flip-Jack, cal'd a Pancake, which ominous incantation the ignorant people doe devoure very greedily."

The piety of such people would seem to have gone sadly astray, for *Shrove* is a word derived from *shrive* which means, to confess; and there was apparently little of that element in the humour of the day, although possibly in the earlier days of the Church such festivities were not so pronounced. Still, they could never have been entirely absent, for Brand informs us that the luxury and intemperance which prevailed were vestiges of the Roman Carnival. The modern pancake, translated from the history of the past, seems to suggest the old saying, "Let us eat, drink, and be merry, for to-morrow we die."

Tossing the Pancake.

The custom of tossing the pancake on Shrove Tuesday is still kept up at Westminster School. It is interesting to compare the difference in details between the celebration in 1790 and 1910. Thus a writer in *The Gentleman's Magazine* 1790 says :— " The under clerk in the College enters the school, and, preceded by the beadle and other officers, throws a large pancake over the bar which divides the upper from the under school.

A gentleman, who was formerly one of the masters of that school, confirmed the ancedote to me, with this alteration, that the cook of the seminary brought it into the school, and threw it over the curtain which separated the forms of the upper from those of the under scholars. I have heard of a similar custom at Eton school."

In Sir Benjamin Stone's *Pictures of National Life and History* we read :—" The ceremony on Shrove Tuesday, though it has been modified slightly from time to time, has remained substantially unaltered for centuries. In the morning one of the vergers from the Abbey, bearing a silver mace, conducts the cook, who carries the pancake in a frying pan, into the great hall where all the boys are assembled. When the room was divided by a curtain, this was then drawn aside, and the cook threw the pancake over the bar towards the door, whereupon all the boys scrambled for it. Of late years only a few—one representing each form chosen by the scholars themselves—have taken part in the scramble. Going forward, the cook hurls the pancake aloft in the direction of the bar.

If it goes clean over, the selected boys make a wild rush for it in an endeavour to catch it whole, and usually failing, then struggle for it on the floor. The one who secures it, or the biggest portion, is entitled to a guinea. The scrimmage is known as the 'greeze.'"

To all appearance there is no great difference in the ceremony as contrasted with that of 1790, but the advent of an Abbey functionary is somewhat peculiar. The Eton custom is thus referred to by Sir Henry Ellis :—" The manuscript in the British Museum, 'Status Scholæ Etonensis, A.D. 1560,' mentions a custom of that school on Shrove Tuesday, of the boys being allowed to play from eight o'clock for the whole day ; and of the cook's coming in and fastening a pancake to a crow, which the young crows are calling upon, near it, at the school door. 'Die Martis Carnis-privii luditur ad horam octavam in totum diem : venit Coquus, affigit laganum Cornici, juxta illud pullis Corvorum invocantibus eum, ad ostium scholæ.' The crows generally have hatched their young at this season."

A modern writer claims that pancakes as a food were first made in Catholic days to use up the eggs and lard that were interdicted during Lent ; and because pancakes were an excellent stay to the appetite while the faithful had to wait long hours in church to be *shrived* by the priest in the confessional. Food made from stale eggs and interdicted lard was no doubt of a quality more useful for sport than digestion, but we shall have to look elsewhere for the origin of the *throwing*. Is it not to be found in the other sports which marked the old-time Pancake Tuesday?—the cock-throwing, the chasing, the

general horse play? Here is a picture of the
festivities over 170 years ago :—

"Battering with massive weapons a cock tied to
a stake, is an annual diversion," says an essayist in
The Gentleman's Magazine (1737), "that for time immemorial has prevailed in this island." A cock has
the misfortune to be called in Latin by the same
word which signifies a Frenchman. "In our wars
with France, in former ages, our ingenious forefathers," says he, "invented this emblematical way
of expressing their derision of, and resentment towards that nation ; and poor Monsieur at the stake
was pelted by men and boys in a very rough and
hostile manner." He instances the same thought at
Blenheim House, where, over the portals, is finely
carved in stone the figure of a monstrous lion tearing
to pieces a harmless cock, which may be justly called
a pun in architecture. "Considering the many ill
consequences," the essayist goes on to observe, "that
attend this sport, I wonder it has so long subsisted
among us. How many warm disputes and bloody
quarrels has it occasioned among the surrounding
mob ! Numbers of arms, legs, and skulls have been
broken by the missive weapons designed as destruction to the sufferer in the string. It is dangerous in
some places to pass the streets on Shrove Tuesday ;
'tis risking life and limbs to appear abroad that day.
It was first introduced by way of contempt to the
French, and to exasperate the minds of the people
against that nation. 'Tis a low, mean expression of
our rage, even in time of war."

One part of this extract is singularly corroborated
by a passage in the *Newcastle Courant* for March 15th,

1783. "Leeds, March 11th, 1783 : Tuesday se'nnight, being Shrove-tide, as a person was amusing himself, along with several others, with the barbarous custom of throwing a cock, at Howdon Clough, near Birstall, the stick pitched upon the head of Jonathan Speight, a youth about thirteen years of age, and killed him on the spot. The man was committed to York Castle on Friday."

The following from an old London newspaper shews that the sport of cock-throwing was then declining. The *London Daily Advertiser*, Wednesday, March 7th, 1759, says : "Yesterday being Shrove Tuesday, the orders of the justices in the City and Liberty of Westminster were so well observed that few cocks were seen to be thrown at, so that it is hoped this barbarous custom will be left off."

Now "throwing" was thus the spirit of the day in the old period ; if they had not had enough fun from throwing at cocks, they pelted prostitutes and hounded them round the town. We can only conclude that throwing the pancake was a sort of kitchen expression of the "sport" of the season.

(6) GOOD FRIDAY : *Hot Cross Buns.*

Every Good Friday morning the baker does a brisk business in hot cross buns, probably with little interest in the origin of the custom, his eye being rather upon the number sold and the accruing profits. There are three points to be considered : they are the three words themselves—buns, cross, and hot. The last mentioned seems to be a mark of modern taste and haste, for in past centuries they were "cross buns" pure and simple. To eat them piping

hot out of the oven is an innovation of comparatively
recent date. The sign of the Cross is easily accounted
for, seeing it was part and parcel of the ritual of
Roman Catholic worship.

In a curious and rare book, entitled *The Canter-
burian's Self-Conviction* (1640), in the Scottish dialect,
no place or printer's name to assist identification,
is this passage : " They avow that signing with the
signe of the Cross at rysing or lying downe, at going
out or coming in, at lighting of candles, closing of
windowes, or any such action, is not only a pious and
profitable ceremonie, but a very apostolick tradition."

Pennant, in his Welsh MS., says : " At the delivery
of the bread and wine at the Sacrament, several,
before they receive the bread or cup, though held out
to them, will flourish a little with their thumb, something like making the figure of the Cross. They do
it (the women mostly) when they say their prayers
on their first coming to church."

Dalrymple, in his *Travels in Spain*, says that there
" not a woman gets into a coach to go a hundred
yards, nor a postilion on his horse, without *crossing*
themselves. Even the tops of tavern bills and the
directions of letters are marked with Crosses."

Among the Irish, when a woman milks her cow,
she dips her fingers into the milk, with which she
crosses the beast, and piously ejaculates a prayer,
saying, " Mary and our Lord preserve thee, until I
come to thee again."

But the origin of " buns " presents a little more
difficulty. Hutchinson, in his *History of Northumberland*, following Mr Bryant's *Antient Mythology*. derives the Good Friday Bun from the sacred Cakes

which were offered at the Arkite Temples, styled
Boun, and presented every seventh day.

Mr Bryant has also the following passage on this
subject :—" The offerings which people in ancient
times used to present to the Gods were generally
purchased at the entrance of the Temple ; especially
every species of consecrated bread, which was de-
nominated accordingly. One species of sacred bread
which used to be offered to the Gods, was of great
antiquity, and called *Boun*. The Greeks, who changed
the *Nu* final into a *Sigma*, expressed it in the nomina-
tive Bous, but in the accusative more truly Boun.
Hesychius speaks of the Boun, and describes it a kind
of cake with a representation of two horns. Julius
Pollux mentions it after the same manner, a sort of
cake with horns. Diogenes Laertius, speaking of the
same offering being made by Empedocles, describes
the chief ingredients of which it was composed. ' He
offered one of the sacred Liba, called a *Bouse*, which
was made of fine flour and honey.' It is said of
Cecrops that *he* first offered up this sort of sweet
bread. Hence we may judge of the antiquity of the
custom from the times to which Cecrops is referred.
The prophet Jeremiah takes notice of this kind of
offering when he is speaking of the Jewish women at
Pathros, in Egypt, and of their base idolatry ; in all
which their husbands had encouraged them. The
women, in their expostulation upon his rebuke, tell
him : ' Did we make her cakes to worship her ? '
Jerem. xliv. 18, 19 ; vii. 18. " Small loaves of bread,"
Mr Hutchinson observes, " peculiar in their form,
being long and sharp at both ends, are called Buns."
These he derives as above, and concludes : " We only

retain the name and form of the *Boun*, the sacred uses
are no more."

It would appear, therefore, as if we have to thank
some Pagan custom for this Good Friday habit of
eating hot cross buns, a custom which, like many
others, was taken over by the Church and Christianised. In these days the religious significance has
been completely lost, and the cross bun is no longer
emblematical of a crucified God. It is an ecclesiastical
remainder which has become a social habit.

(7) GOOD FRIDAY LOAVES.

In some parts of the country it used to be thought,
probably is still thought, wise to retain a loaf baked
on Good Friday, under the impression that it acts as
a charm and a medicinal cure. A writer in *The
Gentleman's Magazine* (1867) says on the subject of
Suffolk superstitions :—" Calling at a cottage one day
I saw a small loaf hanging up oddly in a corner of the
house. I asked why it was placed there, and was told
it was a Good Friday loaf—a loaf baked on Good
Friday ; that it would never grow mouldy (and on
inspecting it I certainly found it very dry) and that it
was very serviceable against some diseases, the bloody
flux being mentioned as an example. Some weeks
afterwards I called again, with a friend, at the same
house, and drew his attention to the loaf which was
hanging in its accustomed corner. The owner of the
house endeavoured to take the loaf down gently, but
failing in the attempt, he gave a violent pull, and the
precious loaf to his dismay was shivered to atoms ;
but in the catastrophe gave us further proofs of its
extraordinary dryness. The old man collected the

fragments and hung them up in a paper bag with all the more reverence on account of the good which the loaf, as he alleged, had done his son. The young man, having been seized with a slight attack of English cholera in the summer, secretly 'abscinded' and ate a piece of the loaf, and when his family expressed astonishment at his rapid recovery, he explained the mystery by declaring that he had eaten of the Good Friday loaf, and had been cured by it."

This is a curious instance of a religious festival day being regarded as able to impart a peculiar consecration to material substances. That the bread should not become mouldy is easily explained by its position ; that it should cure cholera is just as easily understood, for the cure was faith-healing—nothing more, nothing less.

(8) PICKING UP SIXPENCES AT SMITHFIELD.

On Good Fridays at St. Bartholomew's Church, Smithfield, there is a quaint ceremony conducted on a flat tombstone in the churchyard. A churchwarden places twenty-one new sixpences on the tombstone, and twenty-one widows come forward one by one, kneel, and pick up the coins. Afterwards each widow is presented with 2/6. The origin of this ceremony is said to be unknown, although it seems hardly likely that money should be paid out year by year without even a tradition as to its commencement. The surmise that the person who lies buried beneath the tombstone left money to be spent in this way—see Sir Benjamin Stone's remarks in his *Pictures of National Life and History*—only makes the absence of details all the more strange.

(9) EASTER HOLIDAYS.

By the law concerning holidays made in the time
of King Alfred the Great, it was appointed that the
week after Easter should be kept holy. From this
we might safely presume on the true intention of the
Church, namely a time of rejoicing in the spiritual
sense. But in the long run rejoicing tends to assume
one form, i.e. social festivity. Belithus tells us it was
customary in some churches for the Bishops and
Archbishops themselves to play with the inferior
clergy at hand ball, and this, as Durand asserts, even
on Easter Day itself. The Roman Church certainly
erected a standard on Easter Day in token of Christ's
victory, but it would perhaps be indulging fancy too
far to suppose that Bishops and governors of churches
who used to play at hand ball at this season, did it
in a mystical way and with reference to the triumphal
joy of this season. With nations in the state of civilisation in which Europe was found in the early centuries
it is not to be wondered at that an ecclesiastical fact,
intended to be celebrated festively, should assume
the outward expression of an agricultural feast with
all the boisterous freedom of a pagan festival. For
instance there was the custom of *lifting* or *heaving*
at Easter, a custom which took a long time to kill,
and one where it is possible to trace stages of
development from seeming improprieties to respectability. In the Northern counties, as will be
seen, there was a roughness which is absent in the
same custom in London and the South. A writer in
The Gentleman's Magazine (1784) says :—

" *Lifting* was originally designed to represent our

Saviour's resurrection. The men lift the women on Easter Monday, and the women the men on Tuesday. One or more take hold of each leg, and one or more of each arm near the body, and lift the person up, in a horizontal position, three times. It is a rude, indecent, and dangerous diversion, practised chiefly by the lower class of people. Our magistrates constantly prohibit it by the bellman, but it subsists at the end of the town ; and the women have of late years converted it into a money job. I believe it is chiefly confined to these Northern counties."

The following extract is from the *Public Advertiser* for Friday, April 13th, 1787 :—

"The custom of rolling down Greenwich-hill at Easter is a relique of old City manners, but peculiar to the metropolis. Old as the custom has been, the counties of Shropshire, Cheshire, and Lancashire boast one of equal antiquity, which they call Heaving, and perform with the following ceremonies, on the Monday and Tuesday in the Easter week. On the first day, a party of men go with a chair into every house to which they get admission, force every female to be seated in their vehicle, and lift them up three times, with loud huzzas. For this they claim the reward of a chaste salute, which those who are too coy to submit to may get exempted from by a fine of one shilling, and receive a written testimony, which secures them from a repetition of the ceremony for that day. On the Tuesday the women claim the same privilege, and pursue their business in the same manner, with this addition—that they guard every avenue to the town, and stop every passenger, pedestrian, equestrian or vehicular."

That it was not entirely confined, however, to the Northern counties, may be gathered from the following letter, which Mr Brand received from a correspondent of great respectability in 1799 :—

"Dear Sir—Having been a witness lately to the exercise of what appeared to me a very curious custom at *Shrewsbury*, I take the liberty of mentioning it to you, in the hope that amongst your researches you may be able to give some account of the ground or origin of it.   I was sitting alone last Easter Tuesday at breakfast at the Talbot in Shrewsbury, when I was surprised by the entrance of all the female servants of the house handing in an arm chair, lined with white, and decorated with ribbons and favours of different colours.   I asked them what they wanted ?   Their answer was, they came to *heave* me. It was the custom of the place on that morning ; and they hoped I would take a seat in their chair.   It was impossible not to comply with a request very modestly made, and to a set of nymphs in their best apparel, and several of them under twenty.   I wished to see all the ceremony, and seated myself accordingly. The group then lifted me from the ground, turned the chair about, and I had the felicity of a salute from each.   I told them I supposed there was a fee due upon the occasion, and was answered in the affirmative; and, having satisfied the damsels in this respect, they withdrew to *heave* others.   At this time I had never heard of such a custom ; but on inquiry, I found that on Easter Monday, between nine and twelve, the men heave the women in the same manner as on the Tuesday, between the same hours, the women heave the men.   I will not offer any conjecture on the ground of the custom, because I have nothing like data to go upon ; but if you should happen to have heard anything satisfactory respecting it, I should be highly gratified by your mentioning it. I have the honour to be, with much respect, Sir,

Your obedient and faithful servant,

"Basinghall Street,   "THO. LOGGAN.
   May 7, 1799."

But *lifting* was only one of the sports of old Eastertide. There were games on land and water, and much eating and drinking, indeed it was a season *not* kept holy but devoted entirely to merriment. Such are the origins of our own Easter vacations, when for a short spell we visit the seaside and prepare for the work of an arduous summer. To some people the absence of picturesque usage and ceremony is an irreparable loss; to others the absence of vulgar customs and general horse play is a testimony to the advance of civilisation. Certainly it is a pity to lose the picturesque, but on the whole there is more gain than loss in the sober and sombre Easter vacation of to-day as compared with the rollicking past.

(10) BIDDENDEN CAKES.

Hasted, in his *History of Kent*, speaking of Biddenden, tells us that "twenty acres of land, called the Bread and Cheese Land, lying in five pieces, were given by persons unknown, the yearly rents to be distributed among the poor of this parish. This is yearly done on Easter Sunday, in the afternoon, in six hundred cakes, each of which have the figures of two women impressed on them, and are given to

all such as attend the church; and two hundred and
seventy loaves, weighing three pounds and a half
a-piece, to which latter is added one pound and a
half of cheese, are given to the parishioners only, at
the same time. There is a vulgar tradition in these
parts that the figures on the cakes represent the
donors of this gift, being two women, twins, who were
joined together in their bodies, and lived together so
till they were between twenty and thirty years of age.
But this seems without foundation. The truth seems
to be that it was the gift of two maidens of the name
of Preston; and that the print of the women on the
cakes has taken place only within these fifty years,
and was made to represent two poor widows, as the
general objects of a charitable benefaction. An en-
graving of one of these cakes will be found in *Hone's
Every Day Book.*"

These cakes or loaves are still given out on Easter
Sunday, and in Sir Benjamin Stone's *Pictures of
National Life and History* there is a photograph of
the people receiving their cakes.

(11) EASTER EGGS.

The Easter egg is quite as important an item to
the modern manufacturer of toys and sweetmeats as
it was to the ancient religious devotee, who believed
that eggs laid on Good Friday could be kept all the
year, simply because the day itself exercised some
charm on the products of the farmyard. But why an
egg? and why *Easter?* Why is a Christmas egg of
no account at all? Gébélin, author of *The Religious
History of the Calendar,* answers these questions by
saying that all the nations of antiquity—the Egyptians,

Persians, Romans, Greeks, Gauls, and others—regarded
the egg as an emblem of the Universe—a work of the
supreme Divinity. Easter was the time of the solar
New Year—the day of the renewal of all things—the
incubation of Nature. The colouring and ornamenta-
tion of Easter eggs seems to have been part of the
original custom, and was taken over by the Church,
who used red to denote the blood of Christ. The
following statement from Emilianne's *Romish Monks
and Priests* is interesting :—

" On Easter Eve and Easter Day, all the heads of
families send great chargers, full of hard eggs, to the
Church to get them blessed, which the priests perform
by saying several appointed prayers, and making
great signs of the Cross over them, and sprinkling
them with holy water. The priest, having finished
the ceremony, demands how many dozen eggs there
be in every bason?" . . . "These blest eggs have
the virtue of sanctifying the entrails of the body, and
are to be the first fat or fleshy nourishment they take
after the abstinence of Lent. The Italians do not
only abstain from flesh during Lent, but also from
eggs, cheese, butter, and all white meats. As soon as
the eggs are blessed, every one carries his portion
home, and causeth a large table to be set in the best
room in the house, which they cover with their best
linen, all bestrewed with flowers, and place round
about it a dozen dishes of meat, and the great
charger of eggs in the midst. 'Tis a very pleasant
sight to see these tables set forth in the houses
of great persons, when they expose on side-tables
(round about the chamber) all the plate they
have in the house, and whatever else they have that

D

is rich and curious, in honour of their Easter eggs,
which of themselves yield a very fair show, for the
shells of them are all painted with divers colours and
gilt. Sometimes they are no less than twenty dozen
in the same charger, neatly laid together in the form
of a pyramid. The table continues in the same
posture, covered, all the Easter week, and all those
who come to visit them in that time are invited to
eat an Easter egg with them, which they must not
refuse."

As in the case of hot cross buns, the emblem and
the religious idea have become obscured, and this
pagan-Christian relic survives only as a social custom.

(12) KNUTSFORD: THE MAY QUEEN AND THE MORRIS DANCES.

Knutsford enjoys the distinction of celebrating the
custom of crowning the May Queen with an enthusiasm,
an efficiency, and a pictorial splendour which is more
impressive than anything else in the same sphere.
Early in the morning the streets are " sanded " with
brown and white sand in preparation for the procession. All the old characters are present, and many
new ones are imported from time to time, whilst children
in scores eagerly participate. The procession starts
from the Town Hall, and is nearly a mile long; at
the end is the uncrowned Queen. She is chosen by
ballot by the ladies and gentlemen who are responsible
for getting up the demonstration, and the crown
becomes her own property. Circuiting the town, the
procession goes to the Heath, where the actual crowning takes place, followed by games, morris dances,
and the usual festivities, all of which are performed

before the throne—quite an imposing structure in itself.

It is hardly necessary to trace the origin of May festivals in Europe, for all nations have observed them as a mark of joy at the return of the earth to life again. But to show how quickly some of the features of a celebration can drop out of sight, I need only reproduce the following from *The Morning Post*, May 2nd, 1791. The paragraph says that "yesterday, being the 1st of May, according to annual and superstitious custom, a number of persons went into the fields and bathed their faces with the dew on the grass, under the idea that it would render them beautiful. I remember, too, that in walking that same morning between Hounslow and Brentford, I was met by two distinct parties of girls, with garlands of flowers, who begged money of me, saying, ' Pray, sir, remember the Garland.'" The distinctive feature in the festivities at Knutsford, after the coronation, is the Morris dance ; and as this is becoming more popular elsewhere, not so much in the festival as in the social sense, it may be wise to say a word or two on the origin of so interesting a custom. Authorities trace the dance to the Moors—the word *Morisco* being Spanish for a Moor.

The Moorish or Morisco dance was, however, very different from the English form. Douce, in his *Illustrations of Shakespeare and of Ancient Manners*, cites a passage from a play called *Variety* (1649), in which the Spanish Morisco is mentioned, adding that this not only shows the legitimacy of the term *Morris*, but that the real and uncorrupted Moorish dance was to be found in Spain under the name

of Fandango. The Spanish Morrice was also danced
at puppet shows by a person habited like a Moor,
with castagnets ; and Junius has informed us that the
Morris dancers usually blackened their faces with
soot, that they might the better pass for Moors.
Douce goes on to say that " it has been supposed that
the Morris Dance was first brought into England in
the time of Edward the Third, when John of Gaunt
returned from Spain (see Peck's Memoirs of Milton,
p. 135), but it is much more probable that we had
it from our Gallic neighbours, or even from the
Flemings. Few, if any, vestiges of it can be traced
beyond the time of Henry the Seventh, about which
time, and particularly in that of Henry the Eighth,
the Churchwardens' accounts in several parishes
afford materials that throw much light on the subject,
and show that the Morris Dance made a very considerable figure in the parochial festivals."

" We find also that other festivals and ceremonies
had their Morris, as : Holy Thursday ; the Whitsun
Ales ; the Bride Ales or Weddings ; and a sort of
Play, or Pageant, called the Lord of Misrule.
Sheriffs, too, had their Morris Dance."

" The May Games of Robin Hood," it is observed,
" appear to have been principally instituted for the
encouragement of archery, and were generally accompanied by Morris dancers, who, nevertheless,
formed but a subordinate part of the ceremony. It
is by no means clear that, at any time, Robin Hood
and his companions were *constituent* characters in
the Morris. In Laneham's Letter from Kenilworth,
or Killingworth Castle, a Bride Ale is described,
in which mention is made of 'a lively Moris dauns,

according to *the auncient manner* : six dauncerz, Mawd Marion, and the fool.'"

Modern Morris dances are sometimes criticised as to an alleged defect in the number of constituent characters, but it is clear no specific number is necessary, although Maid Marian and the fool are probably as important as any.

(13) FURRY DANCE—HELSTON.

On May 8th every year the inhabitants of Helston celebrate the return of Spring by what is known as the "Furry Dance," to the accompaniment of a quaint horn-pipe tune. A ballad is also sung, and the opening verse is :—

> Robin Hood and Little John,
>   They both are gone to the fair, O,
> And me to the merry green wood,
>   To see what they do there, O.
>   And for to chase, O
>   To chase the buck and doe,
>   With Hal-and-Tow,
>   Jolly rumble, O.

At dawn a band marches through the town, and soon the young people begin to dance in the streets. The "Furry Dance" itself does not "happen" until about 1 p.m. The band begins to play the horn-pipe tune, and the couples trip to the nearest house, waltz through it, and out into the next house, through that, and so on to the next. The band itself actually goes through the houses. There were other ceremonies on Furry Day in bygone years, but the dance alone now survives.

Writing in 1790 a correspondent of *The Gentleman's Magazine* says :—" At Helstone, a genteel and populous borough town in Cornwall, it is customary to dedicate the *eighth* of May to revelry (festive mirth, not loose jollity). It is called the Furry Day, supposed Flora's Day ; not, I imagine, as many have thought, in remembrance of some festival instituted in honour of that goddess, but rather from the garlands commonly worn on that day. In the morning, very early, some troublesome rogues go round the streets with drums, or other noisy instruments, disturbing their sober neighbours ; if they find any person at work, make him ride on a pole, carried on men's shoulders, to the river, over which he is to leap in a wide place, if he can ; if he cannot, he must leap in, tor leap he must, or pay money. About 9 o'clock they appear before the school, and demand a holiday for the Latin boys, which is invariably granted ; after which they collect money from house to house. About the middle of the day they collect together, to dance hand-in-hand round the streets, to the sound of the fiddle, playing a particular tune, which they continue to do till it is dark. This they call a 'Faddy.' In the afternoon the gentility go to some farm-house in the neighbourhood to drink tea, syllabub, etc., and return in a Morris dance to the town, where they form a Faddy, and dance through the streets till it is dark, claiming a right of going through any person's house, in at one door and out at the other. And here it formerly used to end, and the company of all kinds to disperse quietly to their several habitations ; but latterly corruptions have in this, as in other matters, crept in by degrees. The ladies, all elegantly dressed in white muslins, are now conducted by their partners to the ball-room, where they continue their dance till supper-time; after which they all faddy it out of the house, breaking off by degrees to their respective houses. The mobility imitate their superiors, and also adjourn to the several public-houses, where they continue their dance till midnight.   It is, upon the whole, a very festive, jovial, and withal so sober, and, I believe, singular custom ; and any attempt to search out the original of it, inserted in one of your future Magazines, will very much please and gratify DURGAN."

The "original" of it is still wanting—and likely to be. It is one of those obscurities which must be sought, if sought at all, in the local genius of the people.

(14) BAAL FIRE—ST. JOHN'S EVE.

Readers of the Old Testament are well acquainted with the condemnation passed upon the worship of Baal, but some of them may be surprised to know that there is a custom in Northumberland of lighting Baal fires on St. John's Eve, which is a relic of ancient Baal worship. The identity between the celebration of the pagan rite of old and of the modern remainder is too obvious to be doubted. The ancients passed their children through the fire, and the villagers at Whalton used to jump over and through the flames. Moreover, as will be seen from the historical references to be given shortly, there is further ground provided for establishing a genuine fire worship. Of the Whalton custom a modern writer says :—" As midsummer approaches, much wood is marked out for the bonfire, sometimes with the consent of local farmers.

When this has been cut, it is brought into the village with a certain amount of formality. On the evening of the 4th July a cart is borrowed and loaded with branches of faggots, some of the men get into the shafts, more are hooked on by means of long ropes, and then, with a good deal of shouting and horn blowing, the lumbersome vehicle is run down into the village." The same site for the fire is chosen year after year, and it has never been changed. The village turns out *en masse* to see the bonfire built. The children join hands and dance round the stack of wood and branches until they are tired ; youths and maidens also dance a little distance away.

At dark a cry is raised : "Light her!" Soon the whole village is illuminated by a huge blaze, and the Baal fire is at its height. No ceremony follows, but tradition says people used to jump over the fire and through it, a tradition which is well founded, for we have strong evidence of such practices in Scotland and Ireland.

In Sir John Sinclair's *Statistical Account of Scotland* (1794), the minister of Callander, in Perthshire, speaking of "Peculiar Customs," says :—"The people of this district have two customs, which are fast wearing out, not only here but all over the Highlands, and therefore ought to be taken notice of while they remain. Upon the first day of May, which is called *Beltan* or *Bàl-tein*-day, all the boys in a township or hamlet meet in the moors. They cut a table in the green sod, of a round figure, by casting a trench in the ground of such circumference as to hold the whole company. They kindle a fire, and dress a repast of eggs and milk in the consistence of a

custard. They knead a cake of oatmeal, which is
toasted at the embers against a stone. After the
custard is eaten up, they divide the cake into so
many portions, as similar as possible to one another
in size and shape, as there are persons in the company. They daub one of these portions all over
with charcoal until it be perfectly black. They
put all the bits of the cake into a bonnet. Every
one, blindfold, draws out a portion. He who holds
the bonnet is entitled to the last bit. Whoever
draws the black bit is the devoted person who is
to be sacrificed to *Baal*, whose favour they mean to
implore, in rendering the year productive of the
sustenance of man and beast. There is little doubt
of these inhuman sacrifices having been once offered
in this country as well as in the East, although
they now pass from the act of sacrificing, and only
compel the *devoted* person to leap three times through
the flames ; with which the ceremonies of this festival
are closed."

In the same work, the minister of Logierait, in
Perthshire, says :—"On the 1st of May, O. S., a
festival called *Beltan* is annually held here. It is
chiefly celebrated by the cowherds, who assemble
by scores in the fields to dress a dinner for themselves of boiled milk and eggs. These dishes they
eat with a sort of cakes baked for the occasion, and
having small lumps, in the form of nipples, raised
all over the surface. The cake might, perhaps, be
an offering to some deity in the days of Druidism."

Pennant's account in his *Tour in Scotland* (1771)
of this rural sacrifice is more minute. He tells us
that, on the 1st of May, in the Highlands of Scotland,

the herdsmen of every village hold their *Bel-tein.*
"They cut a square trench in the ground, leaving
the turf in the middle ; on that they make a fire of
wood, on which they dress a large caudle of eggs,
butter, oatmeal, and milk, and bring, besides the
ingredients of the caudle, plenty of beer and whisky ;
for each of the company must contribute something.
The rites begin with spilling some of the caudle on
the ground, by way of libation ; on that, every one
takes a cake of oatmeal, upon which are raised nine
square knobs, each dedicated to some particular
being, the supposed preserver of their flocks and
herds, or to some particular animal, the real destroyer
of them. Each person then turns his face to the fire,
breaks off a knob, and, flinging it over his shoulders,
says : ' *This I give to thee, preserve thou my horses ;* '
' *This to thee, preserve thou my sheep ;* ' and so on.
After that they use the same ceremony to the noxious
animals. ' *This I give to thee, O fox! spare thou my
lambs ;* ' ' *this to thee, O hooded crow ;* ' ' *this to thee,
eagle !* '   When the ceremony is over, they dine on
the caudle ; and after the feast is finished, what is
left is hid by two persons deputed for that purpose ;
but on the next Sunday they reassemble and finish
the reliques of the first entertainment." "That the
Caledonians paid a superstitious respect to the sun,
as was the practice among other nations, is evident,"
says Ellis, "not only by the sacrifice at Baltein but
upon many other occasions. When a Highlander
goes to bathe, or to drink waters out of a consecrated
fountain, he must always approach by going round
the place from east to west on the south side in
imitation of the apparent diurnal motion of the sun.

This is called in Gaelic going round the right or the lucky way. And if a person's meat or drink were to affect the wind-pipe, or come against his breath, they instantly cry out *disheal*, which is an ejaculation praying that it may go the right way."

The Baal worship is even more pronounced in Irish history. In *The Survey of the South of Ireland* we read something similar to what has already been quoted in a note from *The Statistical Account of Scotland.* "The sun" (says the writer) "was propitiated here by sacrifices of fire: one was on the 1st of May, for a blessing on the seed sown. The 1st of May is called in Irish language *La Beal-tine*, that is, the day of Beal's fire. Vossius says it is well known that Apollo was called Belinus, and for this he quotes Herodian, and an inscription at Aquileia, *Apollini Belino.* The Gods of Tyre were Baal, Ashtaroth, and all the Host of Heaven, as we learn from the frequent rebukes given to the backsliding Jews for following after Sidonian idols ; and the Phenician Baal, or Baalam, like the Irish Beal, or Bealin, denotes the sun, as Ashtaroth does the moon."

In another place the same author says :—" It is not strange that many Druid remains should still exist ; but it is a little extraordinary that some of their customs should still be practised. They annually renew the sacrifices that used to be offered to Apollo, without knowing it. On Midsummer's Eve, every eminence, near which is a habitation, blazes with Bonfires ; and round these they carry numerous torches, shouting and dancing, which affords a beautiful sight, and at the same time confirms the observation of Scaliger :—' En Irelande ils sont quasi tous papistes, mais c'est Papauté méslee de Paganisme, comme partout.' Though historians had not given us the mythology of the pagan Irish, and though they had not told us expressly that they worshipped Beal, or Bealin, and that this Beal was the Sun and their chief God, it might nevertheless be investigated from this custom, which the lapse of so many centuries has not been able to wear away. . . I have, however, heard it lamented that the alteration of the style had spoiled these exhibitions ; for the Roman Catholics light their Fires by the new style, as the correction originated from a pope ; and for that very same reason the Protestants adhere to the old."

I find the following, much to our purpose, in *The Gentleman's Magazine* for February 1795 :—" The Irish have ever been worshippers of Fire and of Baal, and are so to this day. This is owing to the Roman Catholics, who have artfully yielded to the superstitions of the natives, in order to gain and keep up an establishment, grafting Christianity upón Pagan rites. The chief festival in honour of the Sun and Fire is upon the 21st[1] of June, when the sun arrives at the summer solstice, or rather begins its retrogade motion. I was so fortunate in the summer of 1782 as to have my curiosity gratified by a sight of this ceremony to a very great extent of country. At the house where I was entertained, it was told me that we should see at midnight the most singular sight in Ireland, which was the *lighting of Fires in honour of the Sun.* Accordingly, exactly at midnight, the Fires began to appear ; and taking the advantage of going up to the leads of the house, which had a widely

[1] *Is this not a mistake for the 23rd ?*

extended view, I saw on a radius of thirty miles, all around, the Fires burning on every eminence which the country afforded. I had a farther satisfaction in learning, from undoubted authority, that the people *danced round the Fires*, and at the close went through these fires, and made their sons and daughters, together with their cattle, pass through the Fire ; and the whole was conducted with religious solemnity." This is at the end of some Reflections by the late Rev. Donald M'Queen, of Kilmuir, in the Isle of Skye, on ancient customs preserved in that Island.

The Roman Catholic bishop, Dr Milner, was opposed to the notion of the Irish having ever been worshippers of Fire and of Baal. In *An Inquiry into certain Vulgar Opinions concerning the Catholic Inhabitants and the Antiquities of Ireland* (Lond. 1808), he tells us that the " modern hunters after paganism in Ireland think they have discovered another instance of it (though they derive this neither from the Celtic Druidesses nor the Roman Vestals, but from the Carthaginians or Phœnicians) in the fires lighted up in different parts of the country on the Eve of St. John the Baptist, or Midsummer Day. This they represent as the idolatrous worship of Baal, the Philistine god of Fire, and as intended by his pretended Catholic votaries to obtain from him fertility for the earth. The fact is, these fires, on the eve of the 24th of June, were heretofore as common in England and all over the Continent as they are now in Ireland, and have as little relation with the worship of Baal as the bonfires have which blaze on the preceding 4th of June, being the King's birth-day : they are both intended to be demonstrations of joy. That, however, in honour of Christ's precursor is particularly appropriate, as alluding to his character of bearing witness to the light (John vi. 7) and his being himself a bright and shining light (John v. 35)."

It is only natural that a Christian apologist should take up this attitude, but the verdict of history is against him ; for, in addition to the testimony from Scotland and Ireland, there is similar testimony from England to the actual survivals, one of which has already been noticed.

Borlase in his *Antiquities of Cornwall* tells us:—"Of the fires we kindle in many parts of England, at some stated times of the year, we know not certainly the rise, reason, or occasion, but they may probably be reckoned among the relics of the Druid superstitious Fires.   In Cornwall, the festival Fires, called Bonfires, are kindled on the Eve of St. John the Baptist and St. Peter's Day ; and Midsummer is thence, in the Cornish tongue, called ' Goluan,' which signifies both light and rejoicing.   At these Fires the Cornish attend with lighted torches, tarr'd and pitch'd at the end, and make their perambulations round their Fires, and go from village to village carrying their torches before them ; and this is certainly the remains of the Druid superstition, for ' faces præferre,' to carry lighted torches, was reckoned a kind of Gentilism, and as such particularly prohibited by the Gallick Councils : they were in the eye of the law ' accensores facularum,' and thought to sacrifice to the devil, and to deserve capital punishment."

Echoes of the ceremony are also found in unexpected quarters :—Every Englishman has heard of the " Dance round our coal-fire," which receives

illustration from the probably ancient practice of
dancing round the fires in our Inns of Court (and
perhaps other halls in great men's houses). This
practice was still in 1733 observed at an entertainment at the Inner Temple Hall, on Lord Chancellor
Talbot's taking leave of the house, when " the Master
of the Revels took the Chancellor by the hand, and
he, Mr Page, who with the Judges, Sergeants, and
Benchers, danced round the Coal Fire, according to
the old ceremony, three times ; and all the times the
antient song, with music, was sung by a man in a
Bar gown."

In an old collection of Epigrams and Satires this
leaping over the Midsummer fire is mentioned among
other pastimes :—

> At Shrove—groate, ventor-point or crosse and pile
> *At leaping over a Midsummer bone-fier,*
> Or at the drawing clear out of the myer.[1]

Leaping over the fires is mentioned among the
superstitious rites used at the Palilia in Ovid's *Fasti.*
The Palilia were feasts instituted in honour of Pales,
the goddess of Shepherds on the Calends of May.
But fire ceremonies are not the property of one nation :
they belonged to all, and to-day in Japan it is possible
to see the celebration of fire-walking. From Japan
one may travel to other Continents and see similar
phenomena. As civilisation advances these customs
tend to die down ; but there can be no doubt the few
remaining fire festivals in this country are the relics
of a very old and superstitious worship, which our semi-
savage forefathers indulged in at a time when the sun
and moon were not items of science, but Gods of a

[1] See Reed's edition of Shakespeare, London, 1803, Vol. XX., p. 51.

truth. Christianity was responsible for most of the abolition of these curious practices. For instance, the Sixth Council of Constantinople, A.D. 680, by its 65th canon (cited by Prynne in his *Histriomastix*), has the following interdiction :—" Those Bonefires that are kindled by certaine people on New Moones before their shops and houses, over which also they are ridiculously and foolishly to leape, by a certaine antient custome, we command them from henceforth to cease. Whoever therefore shall doe any such thing ; if he be a clergyman, let him be deposed ; if a layman, let him be excommunicated ; for, in the Fourth Book of the Kings, it is thus written : ' And Manasseh built an altar to all the hoast of heaven, in the two courts of the Lord's house, and made his children to pass through the Fire,' etc."

Prynne—the Puritan stalwart—remarks on this :—" Bonefires therefore had their originall from this idolatrous custome, as this Generall Councell hath defined ; therefore all Christians should avoid them." And the Synodus Francica under Pope Zachary, A.D. 742, cited *ut supra*, inhibits " those sacrilegious Fires which they call *Nedfri* (or Bonefires), and all other observations of the Pagans whatsoever."

A custom that has survived so long in particular places — though few — in England, occasions the enquiry : How have they prevented the death which overtook the celebration elsewhere ? At Whalton the people are more a people to themselves than others, because they are removed from train, tram, and motor bus. By and bye these agents of civilisation will reach them, and the end will be in sight. A new generation with new ideas will spring up, and there will be less disposition to gather the faggots and burn them as the darkness comes down. Finally, Baal fire, even as a fire, will cease to be, and one more custom will pass into history.

(15) HOCKTIDE—OR HOKE DAY.

Hocktide is a very old term used to denote the Monday and Tuesday in the week following the second Tuesday after Easter. The origin of the term and the occasion which gave the festival birth are keenly controverted by antiquarians, and the season itself is now all but forgotten : indeed, if it were not for the fact that Hocktide still survives at Hungerford and other places, it would, like many other customs of the past, find no notice in these pages ; our standpoint being that *survivals* of superstitions and customs are alone of popular interest.

First as to the word itself. Bryant says Hock— the German *Hoch*, and means "a high day." But what made it a high day ? Spelman believed the word came from *hocken*—to bind. He says :— "Hoc day, Hoke day, Hoc-Tuesday, a festival celebrated annually by the English in remembrance of their having ignominiously driven out the Danes, in like manner as the Romans had their Fugalia, from having expelled their kings. He inclines to Lambarde's opinion, that it means 'deriding Tuesday,' as Hocken in German means to attack, to seize, to bind, as the women do the men on this day, whence it is called 'Binding Tuesday.' The origin he deduces from the slaughter of the Danes by Ethelred, which is first mentioned in the Laws of

E

Edward the Confessor, c. 35. He says the day itself is uncertain, and varies, at the discretion of the common people, in different places."

But as the massacre of the Danes took place on Nov. 13—the feast of St. Brice, hocktide could hardly be celebrated in the earlier part of the year. And yet there is a persistent tradition that the Danish massacre was the true origin of hocktide. For instance, Wise in his *Further Observations upon the White Horse* (Oxford, 1742) has collected some interesting evidence. He tells us that the Danes' inhuman behaviour drew upon them at length the general resentment of the English in King Ethelred's reign ; so that in one day (St. Brice's Day A.D. 1001) they were entirely cut off in a general massacre. And, though this did not remain long unrevenged, yet a festival was appointed in memory of it, called *Hoc Tuesday*, which was kept up in Sir Henry Spelman's time, and perhaps may be so in some parts of England. (D. Henr. Spelman, Glossarium, in voce *Hoc-day*.) I find this, among other sports, exhibited at Kenilworth Castle by the Earl of Leicester, for the entertainment of Queen Elizabeth, A.D. 1575. " And that there might be nothing wanting that these parts could afford, hither came the Coventre men, and acted the ancient play, long since used in that city, called HOCKS-TUESDAY, *setting forth the destruction of the Danes in King Ethelred's time*, with which the Queen was so pleas'd, that she gave them a brace of bucks, and five marks in money, to bear the charges of a feast." (Sir Will. Dugdale's Antiq. of Warwickshire, fol. Lond 1656, p. 166.)

This is evidence of considerable weight, and,

although there are other theories of the origin of hocktide, they can produce nothing so substantial. As to the manner of celebrating the event it may be said, in the words of Ellis, that "the expression *Hock*, or *Hoke-tyde*, comprises both days. Tuesday was most certainly the principal day, the *dies Martis ligatoria*. Hoke Monday was for the men, and Hock Tuesday for the women. On both days the men and women, alternately, with great merriment intercepted the public roads with ropes, and pulled passengers to them, from whom they exacted money, to be laid out in pious uses. So that Hoketyde season, if you will allow the pleonasm, began on the Monday immediately following the second Sunday after Easter, in the same manner as several feasts of the dedications of churches, and other holidays, commenced on the day or the vigil before, and was a sort of preparation for, or introduction to, the principal feast."

Some of the entries in the *Lambeth Book* recording hocktyde collections, are very quaint.

"1556—1557. Item of Godman Rundell's wife, Godman Jackson's wife, and Godwife Tegg, for *Hoxce money* by them received *to the use of the Church*, xij*s*." (Archæol. vol. vii. p. 252.)

"1518—1519. Item of William Elyot and John Chamberlayne, for Hoke money gydered in the pareys, iij*s*. ix*d*.

"Item of the gaderyng of *the Churchwardens wyffes on Hoke Mondaye*, viij*s*. iij*d*."

The modern celebration at Hungerford is begun by a watercress supper at the 'John o' Gaunt,'—(he being the patron of the place,) where his wonderful horn, the town's most treasured possession, is kept. The supper consists of black broth, Welsh rarebit, macaroni, and salad, with bowls of punch. Next morning the town crier blows the horn, and the Hocktide court assembles. The jury is sworn, the names of freemen called, and officials elected. The tything or tutti men receive from the constable a pole on the top of which is a tutti or posy. They then go round the town collecting pennies from the men and kisses from the women. Of course there is a lot of "fun," and women make themselves scarce. The crier, poor fellow, is only allowed to collect pennies : kisses are forbidden fruit. When this part of the celebration is over, the Constable (who is chief ruler of the town) gives a luncheon and then holds the Sandon Fee Court for regulating cattle feeding on the Marsh. After another dinner, court leet is held. " Then comes the Constable's banquet, at which his worship sits beneath the famous John o' Gaunt's horn, suspended from the two tutti poles, and the principal feature of which is a toast, ' To the memory of John o' Gaunt.' This is drunk in solemn silence as the clock strikes the midnight hour." And Hocktide is over.[1]

(16) Garland Day at Abbotsbury.

Do we offer floral tributes to Neptune in England to-day ? Yes, at Abbotsbury on the 13th May every year the children go round the village with large garlands, asking for gifts from the inhabitants. When the round has been completed, a start is made for the beach, the flowers are placed in boats, and put

[1] From notes by M. Mc'Donagh in Sir B. Stone's *Pictures etc.*

out to sea—not for Neptune to do as he likes with—
for they are brought back again, taken to the church,
where a service is gone through. Here then is an
excellent instance of a Christianised pagan superstition, for the floral tributes, if Neptune is to be
worshipped, should be committed to the waves. The
idea was to propitiate the god and bring luck in
fishing. In all probability the custom will linger for
some years to come, but it is already robbed of its
original significance, and shows some signs of decay
in consequence. Maybe some modern pagan, inter-
ested in old customs, will induce the inhabitants to
return to the old rite of trusting the floral gifts to
Father Neptune.

(17) Ascension Day—" Beating the Bounds."

The visitor to London, be he a Britisher or a
foreigner, cannot but be struck by the manner in
which the City Corporation keeps up some of the
old customs, particularly those which are carried out
under the eyes of the public. Among them is the
practice of " beating the bounds." Even the callous
man of the City will pause in, say Coleman Street, as
he sees a uniformed servant of the Corporation stop
at a certain point, utter a few words from a document,
and then wait a moment as two or three boys with
bunches of long, thin rods belabour the walls or
doorways to their own satisfaction and the amusement
of the crowd ? What does it all mean ?

It was a general custom formerly (says Bourne),
and is still observed in some country parishes, to go
round the bounds and limits of the parish on one of
the three days before Holy Thursday, or the Feast of

our Lord's Ascension, when the minister, accompanied
by his churchwardens and parishioners, were wont to
deprecate the vengeance of God, beg a blessing on the
fruits of the earth, and preserve the rights and properties of the parish.

He cites Spelman as deriving this custom from the
times of the Heathens, and that it is an imitation
of the Feast called Terminalia, which was dedicated to the god Terminus, whom they considered
as the guardian of fields and landmarks, and the
keeper up of friendship and peace among men.   The
primitive custom used by Christians on this occasion
was for the people to accompany the bishop or some
of the clergy into the fields, where Litanies were
made, and the mercy of God implored, that He would
avert the evils of plague and pestilence, that He would
send them good and seasonable weather, and give them
in due season the fruits of the earth.

In Herbert's *Country Parson* (1652), we are told
that "the Country Parson is a lover of old customs, if
they be good and harmlesse.   Particularly, he loves
Procession, and maintains it, because there are contained therein four manifest advantages.   First, a
blessing of God for the fruits of the field. 2.
Justice in the preservation of bounds. 3. Charitie
in loving, walking, and neighbourly accompanying
one another, with reconciling of differences at that
time, if there be any. 4. Mercie, in relieving the
poor by a liberal distribution and largess, which at
that time is or ought to be used. Wherefore he
exacts of all to be present at the Perambulation, and
those that withdraw and sever themselves from it he
mislikes, and reproves as uncharitable and unneigh-

bourly; and, if they will not reforme, presents them."

This gives a fair notion of the custom in the middle of the seventeenth century. Sir John Hawkins (1776) says in his *History of Music*, " it is the custom of the inhabitants of parishes, with their officers, to perambulate in order to perpetuate the memory of their boundaries, and to impress the remembrance thereof in the minds of young persons, especially boys; to invite boys, therefore, to attend to this business, some little gratuities were found necessary; accordingly it was the custom, at the commencement of the procession, to distribute to each a willow-wand, and at the end thereof a handful of *points*, which were looked on by them as honorary rewards long after they ceased to be useful, and were called Tags."

In the Churchwardens' Accounts of St. Mary-at-Hill in the City of London, 1682, are the following entries:—

	£	s.	d.
" For fruit on Perambulation Day -	1	0	0
For points for two yeres - - -	2	10	0

The following extracts are from the Churchwardens' Books of Chelsea :—

	£	s.	d.
" 1679. Spent at the Perambulation			
Dinner - - - - - - -	3	10	0
Given to the boys that were whipt -	0	4	0
Paid for poynts for the boys - -	0	2	0

(Lysons's Environs of London,
vol. ii. p. 126.)

The second of these entries alludes to another expedient for impressing the recollection of particular boundaries on the minds of some of the young people.

"Bumping persons to make them remember the parish boundaries has been kept up even to this time (1830). See a trial on the occasion, where an angler was bumped by the parishioners of Walthamstow parish, reported in the Observer Newspaper of January 10th, 1830. He was found angling in the Lea, and it was supposed that bumping a stranger might probably produce an independent witness of parish boundary. He obtained £50 damages."

The encroaching of boundaries is now an item against which it is superfluous to obtain protection, and all that remains of a once important custom is the quaint journey round the City of London previously referred to, and the repetition of similar functions in Linlithgow and Selkirk, also the Tower of London.

(18) Ascension Day—Other Superstitions.

W. C. Hazlitt quotes from *The Times* of 1888 an interesting account of the Penrhyn quarrymen:—
"Yesterday, being Ascension Day, work was entirely suspended at Lord Penrhyn's extensive slate quarries near Bangor. The cessation of work is not due to any religious regard for the day, but is attributable to a susperstition, which has long lingered in the district, that if work is continued an accident is inevitable. Some years ago the management succeeded in overcoming this feeling, and in inducing the men to work. But each year there was a serious accident, and now

all the men keep at a distance from the quarries on Ascension Day." It is difficult to account for this attitude on the part of the quarrymen, except that they are, by heredity and instinct, a superstitious race, well able to establish a local cult of their own. There is admittedly some logic in the argument that since Ascension Day has been a time of holiday festivity, at first religious, and afterwards secular, therefore work on that day savours of sacrilege. But in view of the immunity from accidents in other callings, it is not remarkable that fatalities should occur in somewhat dangerous occupations like quarrying.

Penrhyn is not alone in having a local superstition, or, perhaps, I ought to say, a custom based on an old superstition. Sir Henry Ellis says Shaftesbury had its own method of celebration (probably now discontinued), wherein the inhabitants paid a yearly tribute of acknowledgment to the Lord of Gillingham Manor for the water supplied from his estate. The tribute took the form of a calf's head and pair of gloves. "Riding the Marches" is said to be still prevalent in Scotland, and is celebrated on the day after Whitsunday fair by the Magistrates and Burgesses, called the Landsmark, or Langemark Day, from the Saxon *Langemark*. At Tissington, County Derby, the inhabitants were wont to decorate their well on Ascension Day.

(19) ALL FOOLS' DAY.

The unsuspecting City man who, on the point of commencing his day's work at 10 a.m. on any April 1st, receives a 'phone message from a friend desiring

an immediate interview on important business, sets
out at once for the place of meeting, only to find that
the friend knows nothing about it, and has actually
had no occasion to use the 'phone at all up to that
moment. Then the City man remembers the date,
and realises that he has been fooled. It is still early,
just 10.30 a.m., and he begins to take his revenge
on other friends, until things may be said to "hum."
But whilst the fun is fast and furious, very few of these
practical jokers can say how the custom of fooling on
this day arose ; and if one turns to his handy Encyclopædia for information, he will read that "it is of
unknown antiquity."

As might be expected, some writers attempt to
trace the origin to a Nature feast—that of the Vernal
Equinox—and through Nature to a starting point in
Christian history. Maurice, in his *Indian Antiquities*
(vol VI., p. 71) speaks of the first of April as the
ancient feast of the Vernal Equinox, equally observed
in India and Britain. He goes on to say that the
date was held as a high and general festival, "in
which an unbounded hilarity reigned through every
order of its inhabitants; for the sun at that period
of the year, entering into the sign Aries, the New
Year, and with it the season of rural sports and
vernal delight, was then supposed to have commenced. The proof of the great antiquity of the
observance of this annual festival, as well as the
probability of its original establishment in an Asiatic
region, arises from the evidence of facts afforded
us by astronomy. Although the reformation of the
year by the Julian and Gregorian Calendars, and the
adaptation of the period of its commencement to a

different and far nobler system of theology, have
occasioned the festival sports, anciently celebrated
in this country on the first of April, to have long
since ceased; and although the changes occasioned,
during a long lapse of years, by the shifting of the
Equinoctial points, have in Asia itself been productive of important astronomical alterations, as to
exact æra of the commencement of the year; yet,
on both Continents, some very remarkable traits of
the jocundity which then reigned, remain even to
these distant times. Of those preserved in Britain,
none of the least remarkable or ludicrous is that relic
of its pristine pleasantry, the general practice of
making April-Fools, as it is called, on the first day
of that month; but this, Colonel Pearce (Asiastic
Researches, vol. II., p. 334) proves to have been
an immemorial custom among the Hindoos, at a
celebrated festival holden about the same period in
India, which is called *the Huli Festival.* ' During the
Huli, when mirth and festivity reign among the
Hindoos of every class, one subject of diversion is
to send people on errands and expeditions that are
to end in disappointment, and raise a laugh at the
expense of the person sent. The Huli is always
in March, and the last day is the general holiday.
I have never yet heard any account of the origin
of this English custom; but it is unquestionably very
ancient, and is still kept up even in great towns,
though less in them than in the country. With us,
it is chiefly confined to the lower class of people; but
in India high and low join in it; and the late Suraja
Doulah, I am told, was very fond of making Huli
Fools, though he was a Mussulman of the highest

rank. They carry the joke here so far as to send letters making appointments, in the names of persons who it is known must be absent from their houses at the time fixed upon ; and the laugh is always in proportion to the trouble given.' The least inquiry into the ancient customs of Persia, or the minutest acquaintance with the general astronomical mythology of Asia, would have told Colonel Pearce that the boundless hilarity and jocund sports prevalent on the first day of April in England, and during the Huli Festival of India, have their origin in the ancient practice of celebrating with festival rites the period of the Vernal Equinox, or the day when the new year of Persia anciently began."

Thus it would appear that All Fools' Day is not a British or even a continental monopoly, for the French "Poisson d'Avril" owes its existence to the same cause as our own. But why "All" Fools' Day? "All" is said by some authorities to be a corruption of "auld," i.e. old, mention being found in the Romish calendar of a "Feast of Old Fools." (Auldborough, in Yorkshire, now Aldborough, is always pronounced *All*borough.) But this feast was held on January 1st, and although removals of feasts were not unknown in the crowded state of the Roman calendar, the theory that the ancient Druids were the old fools, whom the new Christians taunted and set apart for a day of "mafficking," is hardly tenable. The Christian interpretation is given by Bellingen in his *Etymology of French Proverbs*. The word "poisson" in the phrase "poisson d'Avril" is his starting point.

"Poisson," he contends, is corrupted through the ignorance of the people from "Passion"; and length of time has almost totally defaced the original intention, which was as follows : that as the Passion of our Saviour took place about this time of the year, and as the Jews sent Christ backwards and forwards to mock and torment him, i.e. from Annas to Caiaphas, from Caiaphas to Pilate, from Pilate to Herod, and from Herod back again to Pilate, this ridiculous or rather impious custom took its rise from thence, by which we send about from one place to another such persons as we think proper objects of our ridicule.

This is rather too ingenious to be convincing. The most natural suggestion was made by Dr. Pegge, Rector of Whittington, in *The Gentleman's Magazine* for April, 1766. After discussing the theories previously outlined, he says :—" Now, thirdly, to account for it ; the name undoubtedly arose from the custom, and this, I think, arose from hence : our year formerly began, as to some purposes and in some respects, on the 25th of March, which was supposed to be the Incarnation of our Lord ; and it is certain that the commencement of the new year, at whatever time that was supposed to be, was always esteemed an high festival, and that both amongst the antient Romans and with us. Now great festivals were usually attended with an Octave (see *Gentleman's Magazine*, 1762, p. 568), that is, they were wont to continue eight days, whereof the first and last were the principal ; and you will find the 1st of April is the octave of the 25th of March, and the close or ending, consequently, of that feast, which was both the Festival of the Annunciation and of the New Year. From hence, as I take it, it became a day of extraordinary mirth and festivity, especially amongst the lower sorts, who are apt to pervert and make a bad use of institutions which at first might be very laudable in themselves."

(20) LICHFIELD GREENHILL BOWER.

In the early days of England, when the nation was being organised for defence, it was incumbent upon every town and village to hold an annual meeting to consider the defence of the country against "all foreigners and enemies." This regulation is maintained in the Laws of Edward the Confessor. Other and later acts specify what the town must provide by way of the implements of war. Of course these duties now devolve upon a government department, but at Lichfield, in June, the city still holds its annual meeting, and boys are paraded, wearing the suits of armour provided ·for defence against the invasion of Germany! The function is carried out with dignity, as becomes the remembrance of an old custom, but when it is over the day is given up to jollity of the true English type.

(21) LAMMAS DAY.

Lammas Day seems to have been a great day of accounts in early British history; it is still a quarter day in Scotland. The origin of the word is much disputed. A writer in 1754 says :—"Our ancestors distributed the year into four quarters, Candlemas, Whitsuntide, Lammas, and Martinmas ; and this was every whit as common as the present division of Lady Day, Midsummer, Michaelmas, and Christmas. Lammas was the specific day whereon Peter's

Pence, most rigorously collected, was paid. It was
thus a day of accounts, and 'latter Lammas' means
last day of accounts." The 1st of August was called
Lammas because, some authorities say, the priests
were then wont to gather their tithe lambs ; others
derive it from the Saxon word *Leffmesse* i.e. bread
mass, it being kept as a thanksgiving for the first
fruits of the corn. It is also called *gule* or yule of
August in old almanacs. Mr G. L. Gomme in *The
Antiquary* has thus summarised the available facts :—
"Lammas Day is properly the 1st of August. The
Act of George II., which established the new style in
England, excepted the days for the commencement
of Lammas nights from the operation of the Statute.
Lammas Day under this operation is now the 13th
of August. It is one of the four cross quarter days
as they are now called. Whitsuntide was formerly
the first of these quarters, Lammas the second,
Martinmas the next, and Candlemas the last. Such
partition of the year was once as common as the
present divisions of Lady Day, Midsummer, Michaelmas, and 'Xmas. Some rents are still payable on
those ancient quarter days in England, and they were
not long ago, even if they do not still continue,
general in Scotland. It is a day on which many
quaint customs were enacted ; but the one great
custom, which marks it as a link with a very remote
past, is the removal of the fences from many lands
throughout the country, and the throwing open to
common pasturage of lands which, till this day from
the end of last Lammastide, had been used as private
property. In fact it is not too much to say that in
this custom of Lammastide we have the key to the

whole system of ancient agriculture. Wherever we find Lammas customs in England, we may take it for granted that it is the last remaining link of a whole group of customs which together make up the history of the primitive village community. It is curious to observe with what varying degrees of integrity customs have lived in various parts of the country. In some places, for instance, we may find only the bare mention of Lammastide, and the throwing down of fences and the consequent opening of land to common. In other places there is much more at the back of this Lammas customs—there is sufficient to enable us to open the great book of comparative politics and to take our studies to that ancient Aryan land, India, or even still further back in the history of primitive society, the native savages of Africa."

(22) HARVEST HOME—THE KERN BABY.

Macrobius tells us that among the ancients the farmers, when they got in their harvest, were wont to feast with their servants who had laboured with them in tilling the ground. So in later centuries when Europe had, for the most part, become christianised, the Harvest Home was a real celebration, master and servant sat at the same table, and, when the feasting was over, they spent the remainder of the night in dancing and singing. Such a custom has obviously a natural origin in the gladness of having sown and reaped, and stored the corn in the granary ; there is an end of anxiety about sun, and weather, and blight, and all the ills affecting him who is at the mercy of the heavens.

Not much is left to us of the old Harvest Home.

Grain growing is nowadays part and parcel of commerce ; and railways and steamships have turned the channel of its romance from one of poetry into science. In England the farmer is as glad as the Roman, or the Hebrew of old, to gather in his crops under a benevolent sky, but he feels that the Harvest Home belongs to another age, and so the church has taken the festival out of his hands. The modern Harvest Thanksgiving service is about all that is left to us of one of the most natural and simple of customs —one belonging to no nation alone, but belonging to man as man.

In a few places, however, there are remnants of the old festival still left, and among others Whalton still holds the chief place. Here they still make and display the Kern Baby. A photograph of a recent baby is given in Sir Benjamin Stone's *Pictures*. Kern, or Cheorn, is said to come from the Icelandic *Kirna*— the feast of harvest home, so called because a churnful of cream formed an important part of the entertainment. Thus Scott in *Marmion* says :—

His rustic Kirn's loud revelry.

The Kern baby is an image dressed up with corn and carried before the reapers to the harvest home. This derivation is rather fanciful, and the most obvious explanation is that Kern is a corruption of *corn*. Hutchinson in his *History of Northumberland* is of this opinion.

" An old woman, who in a case of this nature is respectable authority, at a village in Northumberland informed me that, not half a century ago, they used everywhere to dress up something similar to the figure above described at the end of Harvest, which

F

was called a Harvest Doll, or *Kern Baby*. This northern word is plainly a corruption of Corn Baby, or Image, as is the *Kern* Supper, which we shall presently consider, of Corn Supper. In Carew's Survey of Cornwall, p. 20 b, ' an ill kerned or saved Harvest' occurs."

Speaking of the custom itself, he adds :—" In some places, an Image apparelled in great finery, crowned with flowers, a sheaf of corn placed under her arm, a scycle in her hand, carried out of the village in the morning of the conclusive reaping day, with musick and much clamour of the reapers, into the field, where it stands fixed on a pole all day, and when the reaping is done, is brought home in like manner. This they call the Harvest Queen, and it represents the Roman Ceres."

In Kent the custom took another form, that of the *Ivy Girl*, " which is a figure composed of some of the best corn the field produces, and made as well as they can into a human shape ; this is afterwards curiously dressed by the women, and adorned with paper trimmings, cut to resemble a cap, ruffles, handker-chief, etc. of the finest lace. It is brought home with the last load of corn from the field upon the waggon, and they suppose entitles them to a supper at the expense of their employers."

In Scotland, according to the *Statistical Account* (1797), the custom was to make a figure called *the Maiden*. In Longforgan, Perthshire, it was " till very lately, the custom to give what was called *a Maiden Feast*, upon the finishing of the Harvest ; and to prepare for which, the last handful of Corn reaped in the field was called *the Maiden*. This was generally contrived to fall into the hands of one of the finest girls in the field, was dressed up with ribands, and brought home in triumph with the music of fiddles or bagpipes. A good dinner was given to the whole band, and the evening spent in joviality and dancing, while the fortunate lass who took the Maiden was the Queen of the Feast ; after which this handful of Corn was dressed out generally in the form of a Cross, and hung up with the date of the year, in some conspicuous part of the house. This custom is now entirely done away, and in its room each shearer is given 6d, and a loaf of bread. However, some farmers, when all their Corns are brought in, give their servants a dinner and a jovial evening, by way of Harvest Home."

The tendencies of the Protestant Reformation were so distinctly averse to images of any description that we must look to the quarrels of religious leaders for the cause of the decay in Harvest Festivals. So far back as 1602 Newton, in his *Tryall of a Man's Owne Selfe*, when speaking of breaches of the Second Commandment, says :—" the *adorning with garlands*, or *presenting unto any image of any Saint, whom thou has made speciall choise of to be thy patron and advocate, the firstlings of thy increase, as* CORNE *and* GRAINE, and other oblations."

Puritanism, and art, and poetry, do not dwell together.

(23) HALLOWEEN.

Hallow Even is the vigil of All Saints' Day, which is on the first of November. Christian history presents a curious divergence of custom in regard to this Church festival ; for whilst in Catholic countries the faithful turn their steps to the churchyard and place flowers on the graves of the departed, the Protestant section, and that portion of the community known as worldly people, celebrate the occasion by making merry and using various means to peer into the future. All Saints' Day being originally a day for remembering the souls of the departed, it is confessedly difficult to trace any connection between a pious instruction on the part of the Church, and the old (and modern) practice of unmarried women, who use this day—or eve—to divine their matrimonial bliss, or misery. But as with so many Church festivals the jollity and the seriousness often went together, or the directly religious act preceded the merry-making ; and in the course of time the religious element grew weaker, whilst the secular element retained more or less its vitality. Anyhow in the North of England the sanctity of Hallow Even became transmogrified into " Nut Crack Night." Girls anxious, or, shall I say, curious, to know the name of their husbands, would place two nuts in the fire side by side, giving them names. If the fire caused the nuts to burst and fly apart, the sign was distinctly bad ; if they burned together, the omen was decidedly good. Gay in his *Spell* thus refers to the custom :—

> " Two hazel nuts I threw into the flame,
> And to each nut I gave a sweetheart's name :
> This with *the loudest bounce* me sore amaz'd,
> That in a *flame of brightest colour* blaz'd ;
> As *blaz'd the nut*, so *may thy passion grow*,
> For 'twas thy Nut that did so brightly glow ! "

" In marriage ceremonies among the Romans the bridegroom threw nuts about the room for the boys

to scramble. The epithalamiums of the classics confirm this, and Horace speaks of the use of nuts in
sports. They were not excluded from the catalogue
of superstitions under Papal Rome. Thus on the
10th of August in the Romish ancient Calendar I find
it observed that some religious use was made of them,
and that they were in great estimation : Nuces in
pretio et religiosæ."

(24) THE FIFTH OF NOVEMBER.

It is instructive to note how little influence the
origin of this celebration has on the observance of
the custom. There is no question of Roman
Catholicism *versus* Protestantism ; no preaching in
churches against the papists ; no defiance of Protestant practice. Gunpowder Plot is an item familiar
to every schoolboy who has read his history-book,
but the religious significance is a mere nothing compared with the fun of firing off fireworks. And I
question whether even that will last another century ;
for whereas once—not thirty years ago—every part
of the countryside would be alight with huge fires,
one can now only note their slow decay ; and the
sale of fireworks is not on the increase. Perhaps it
is just as well. If the function is religious, it should
be religiously observed ; if not, let it become what it
has become—the one day in the year when we agree
to let off our squibs and crackers. " The search for
Guy Fawkes " is still kept up as a formal custom.

(25) WROTH MONEY.

Brand does not appear to have noticed this
interesting custom, and for the following paragraphs

I am indebted to Sir Benjamin Stone's *Pictures of National Life and History*, with notes by Michael McDonagh. Speaking of the ceremony at Knightlow Cross, he says :—" A tribute which dates back for 1,000 years, and connects the present with that remote past, when the central counties of England were for the most part a wild and uncultivated chase, is rendered on Knightlow Hill, near Dunchurch, Warwickshire, on the early morn of St. Martin's Day. Known as 'wroth money,' it is paid to the Duke of Buccleuch, as an acknowledgment of certain concessions made by his ancestors on pain of a forfeit for every penny of 20s. or 'a white bull with red nose and red ears.' Before dawn on St. Martin's Day, representatives of the townships which owe tribute, as well as crowds of spectators, wend their way to Knightlow Hill from all points of the compass. There on the summit, and close to the Holyhead Road, they gather round the base of an old cross. The Duke's agent then reads out the name of the parishes and hamlets which are called upon to make payments, whereupon the persons responsible for such dues drop their coins into the hollow of a large stone. In all there are 25 places which have to pay wroth money, the amount ranging from 1d. to 2s. 3½d. The whole amount due (only 9s. 4d.) is usually collected, though within recent years there have been defaulters on several occasions. Once during the last century the prescribed penalty for nonpayment was enforced. When the collection is completed and the Duke's agent has checked the names on the list, the company adjourn to the village inn, which by its sign, the 'Dun Cow,' helps to perpetuate the legend of the slaying of the gigantic dun cow by Guy, Earl of Warwick. Here breakfast is served at the Duke's expense to those who have made payment, and subsequently the whole company, long churchwarden pipes in hand, drink his grace's health in tumblers of rum and milk. . . . In an ancient charter preserved in Broughton House, Northamptonshire—a charter which has only once been challenged, and having then (in 1685) been confirmed, has since remained undisputed—wroth money is merely declared to be a legal tribute for ancient privileges, the nature of those privileges not being defined."

(26) CHRISTMAS.

Christianity became civilly established in the fourth century, and the festivals held in honour of Bacchus and other heathen deities at the Christmas season of the year gradually fell into decay. The primitive teachers of the Christian religion prohibited these scenes of festivity as being unsuited to the character of their founder, but on the formation of a regular hierarchy, supported by political power, the introduction of particular festivals, adapted to the respective periods of the pagan ones, soon became general. Thus by adopting the obsolete feasts of the Greeks and Romans, and adapting them to the most striking events in the lives of Christ and his notable followers, the prejudices of the pagan worshippers were shaken, and numerous converts obtained. Unfortunately these festival saint days at length became so numerous under the Papal authority, that the days of the year were not sufficiently numerous for their celebration. However, since the Reformation, the far greater portion have sunk into oblivion, and are only known by referring to the old calendars of the Saints. Yet the principal ones commemorated in honour of Christ are still retained, though not celebrated with the same festivity and show as in former times. Among these Christmas Day may be considered the most important. The first festival of this kind ever held in Britain, it is said, was celebrated by King Arthur in the city of York, A.D. 521. Previously to this year the 25th of December was dedicated to Satan, or to the heathen deities worshipped during the dynasties of the British, Saxon, and Danish Kings. In the year 521 this chivalrous monarch won the battle of Badan Hills, when 90,000 (?) of the enemy were slain, and the city of York was delivered up to him. He took up his winter quarters there, and held the festival of Christmas. The churches which lay levelled to the ground he caused to be rebuilt, and the vices attendant on heathenish feasts were banished from York for ever. As if in memory of its origin this county, Yorkshire seems to preserve the festivities of Christmas with more ancient hospitality than any other part of Great Britain. But everywhere the spirit of Christmas festivity has been broken; the old customs die one by one, and Yuletide is now, much more a general holiday, with plum pudding, presents, and paid bills as specialities, than anything religious and historic.

CHRISTMAS DECORATIONS.

The custom of decorating churches, streets, and private houses with holly and evergreens at Christmas still prevails among us; and in these decorations mistletoe occupies a place of peculiar significance. Vergil compares the golden bough in Infernis to the misletoe, and there is evidence that the use of this plant-parasite was not unknown to the ancients in their religious ceremonies, particularly the Greeks, of whose poets Vergil was the acknowledged imitator. It is certain that misletoe was held in high respect by the Northern nations of Europe, the Celts and the Goths being distinctive in their veneration about the time of the year when the Sun approaches the Winter Solstice. That the Druids in Britain regarded misletoe with a religious eye is too well-known to need further remark; but they were accustomed to decorate at 'Xmas time with all kinds of green plants, and the Church took over this practice, in some cases making an exception of the misletoe. Brand, however, is of opinion, although Gay mentions the misletoe among those evergreens that were *put up in Churches*, it never entered these sacred edifices but by mistake, or ignorance of the sextons; for it was the heathenish or profane plant, as having been of such distinction in the pagan rites of Druidism, and it therefore had its place assigned it in kitchens, where it was hung up in great state with its white berries; and whatever female chanced to stand under it, the young man present either had a right or claimed one of saluting her, and of plucking off a berry at each kiss. " I have made many diligent inquiries after the truth of this. I learnt, at Bath, that it never came into church there. An old sexton at Teddington in Middlesex informed me that some misletoe was once put up in the church there, but was by the clergyman immediately ordered to be taken away."

Over against this opinion must be put that of Stukeley in his *Medallic History of Carausius*, where he mentions the introduction of misletoe into York Cathedral on Christmas Eve as a remain of Druidism. Speaking of the Winter Solstice, our Christmas, he says : "This was the most respectable festival of our Druids, called Yule-tide ; when misletoe, which they called *All-heal*, was carried in their hands and laid on their altars, as an emblem of the salutiferous advent of Messiah. This misletoe they cut off the trees with their upright hatchets of brass, called Celts, put upon the ends of their staffs, which they carried in their hands. Innumerable are these instruments found all over the British Isles.

"The custom is still preserved in the North, and was lately at York : on the Eve of Christmas-Day *they carry Misletoe to the high Altar of the Cathedral, and proclaim a public and universal liberty, pardon, and freedom to all sorts of inferior and even wicked people at the gates of the city, towards the four quarters of Heaven.*"

The policy of the early Christian ecclesiastic seems to have been that of accepting prevalent customs by giving them a Christian interpretation ; but where a complete acceptance might defeat his purpose, he drew a hard and fast line of separation. Thus Brand refers to the Council of Bracara as forbidding

Christians to deck their houses with bay leaves and green boughs, but this prohibition extended only to their doing it at the same time as the Pagans. The use of misletoe in churches, a Druid sacred plant, might easily injure the faith of the members, so that its prohibition in some centres is easily understood. But an unusual plant, once put to unusual and withal religious uses cannot easily lose its position in human ceremonial; and when we find it in the home for osculatory purposes—the essence of the misletoe idea to-day—we can without much imagination see how the change came about. Stow in his *Survey of London* supplies an interesting picture of 'Xmas decorations in the past centuries. He says that "against the Feast of Christmas every man's house, as also their parish churches, were decked with holme, ivy, bayes, and whatsoever the season of the year afforded to be green. The conduits and standards in the streets were likewise garnished; among the which I read that in the year 1444 by tempest of thunder and lightning, towards the morning of Candlemas Day, at the Leadenhall in Cornhill, a Standard of tree, being set up in the midst of the pavement, fast in the ground, nailed full of holme and ivie, for disport of Christmass to the people, was torne up and cast down by the malignant Spirit (as was thought), and the stones of the pavement all about were cast in the streets, and into divers houses, so that the people were sore aghast at the great tempests."

Bourne observes that this custom of adorning the windows at this season with bay and laurel is but seldom used in the North; but in the South, particularly at our Universities, it is very common to deck not only the common windows of the town, but also the chapels of the colleges, with branches of laurel, which was used by the ancient Romans as the emblem of Peace, Joy, and Victory. In the Christian sense it may be applied to the victory gained over the Powers of Darkness by the coming of Christ.

(27) CHRISTMAS BOXES.

The dustman, the turncock, the postman, and the tradesman's boy expect their Christmas boxes at Christmas time, but they could not explain the origin of the custom, and would not if they could. It is a money collecting season for them, and the more they can rake in the better they like it. A handful of silver is worth a good deal of book knowledge about Christmas boxes in the past.

One writer says:—" The Romish Priests had masses said for almost everything: if a ship went out to the Indies, the priest had a box in her, under the protection of some saint: and for masses, as their cant was, to be said for them to that saint, etc. the poor people must put something into the Priest's Box, which was not opened till the ship's return. The mass at that time was called Christmas: the box called Christmas Box, or money gathered against that time, that masses might be made by the priests to the saints to forgive the people the debaucheries of that time: and from this, servants had the liberty to get box money, that they too might be enabled to pay the priests for his masses knowing well the truth of the proverb. ' No penny :

no Pater-nosters'." If this be the true origin, the modern custom appears to be a strange perversion of the primary intention. But we find that barbers' shops used to be supplied with a box on the wall into which every customer put something; the presumption being that these thrift boxes, as they were called, had no ecclesiastical purpose in view, their associations being secular—even selfish, in a non-depreciatory sense. So also Gay in his *Trivia* says:

> "Some boys are rich by birth beyond all wants,
> Beloved by uncles, and kind, good, old aunts;
> When Time comes round a *Christmas Box* they bear,
> And one day makes them rich for all the year."

Christmas boxing was apparently a youth's prerogative in those days, just as it used to be in the early nineteenth century.

But it is possible to trace the custom beyond the border line of the earliest Roman Christianity, to the Roman Paganalia instituted by Servius Tullius and celebrated in the beginning of the year. An altar was erected in every village where persons gave money. The apprentices' boxes were formerly made of pottery, and Aubrey mentions a pot in which Roman denarii were found resembling in appearance an apprentices' earthen Christmas box.[1] Professor E. B. Tylor, in his *Primitive Culture* is of opinion that the customs of Yuletide reveal a heathen if not invariably a solar origin. Christmas boxes—and of course *Boxing Day* is the day when the boxes were opened and the money distributed—

[1] *Gentleman's Magazine*, 1828. Earthen Christmas boxes are referred to in Browne's *A Map of the Microcosme* (1642).

were a duplicate of Roman gifts called *strenæ*. The practice of giving Christmas presents is of later date.

(29) YULE LOGS

There seem to be a hundred origins of the word *Yule* according to the writers on popular antiquities. The most ingenious is that of Bryant, who derives the Feast *Juul* or *Yule* from a Hebrew word—*Lile*, Night. *Lile*, he adds, is formed from a verb signifying to *howl*, because at that time, *i.e.* at night, the beasts of the forest go about howling for their prey. "In the Northern counties, nothing is more common than to call that melancholy barking dogs oft make in the night *Yowling*, and which they think generally happens when some one is dying in the neighbourhood."

Christmas Day, in the primitive Church, was always observed as the Sabbath day, and like that, preceded by an Eve, or Vigil. Hence our present Christmas Eve.

On the night of this eve our ancestors were wont to light up candles of an uncommon size, called Christmas candles, and lay a log of wood upon the fire, called a Yule-clog, or Christmas-block, to illuminate the house, and, as it were, to turn night into day. This custom is in some measure still kept in the North of England.

The following occurs in Herrick's *Hesperides* :—

CEREMONIES FOR CHRISTMASSE.
" Come bring with a noise,
My merry, merrie boys,
    The Christmass Log to the firing :
While my good Dame she
Bids ye all be free,
    And drink to your heart's desiring.

" *With the last year's Brand*
 Light the new Block and,
   For good successe in his spending,
 On your psaltries play,
 That sweet luck may
   Come while the Log is teending.

" Drink now the strong beere,
 Cut the white loaf here,
   The while the meat is a-shredding
 For the rare mince-pie,
 And the plums stand by
   To fill the paste that's a-kneading."

Christmas, says Blount, was called the Feast of Lights in the Western or Latin Church, because they used many lights or candles at the feast ; or rather because Christ, the light of all lights, that true light, then came into the world. Hence the Christmas candle, and what was, perhaps, only a succedaneum, the Yule-block, or clog, before candles were in general use. Thus a large coal is often set apart at present, in the North, for the same purpose, *i.e.* to make a great light on Yule or Christmas Eve. Lights, indeed, seem to have been used upon all festive occasions, e.g. our illuminations and fire-works, on the news of victories.

In *The Gentleman's Magazine* for 1790 a writer traces the Yule log to the *Cyclops* of Euripides. (See Act I, sc I).

(29) LUCKY AND UNLUCKY DAYS.

Should a City man of the present day meet another City man, and in the course of conversation ask the question : " What is your lucky day ? " there would be no surprise on the face of the answerer. Perhaps he would shrug his shoulders, as if to say, " I have no theory on the matter," but the notion in itself would not be entertained as absurd. Most of us in our experience have noticed, or we *think* we have noticed that certain days never bring any luck, rather otherwise ; and, following feeling instead of thought, we put off the inauguration of important enterprises until a more convenient season. This attitude does not suggest mental feebleness—it is an attitude taken up by some of the smartest men in commerce and finance. They do not care a straw whether people laugh at them or not ; their experience has indicated that certain seasons, certain days, certain months, are never propitious ; and without considering other people's opinions for one moment, they pursue their own course. One man I know passed through several severe losses and difficulties, all of which occurred in the November of the fatal years : nobody could convince him that every day in every November was not dead against his interests, although he was in other respects of quite normal judgment. I am of opinion there is no truth in the luck or unluck of days, but the truth of the superstition is not the point. How did it originate : that is the question ? And why does it persist ? Before me I have a sort of guide to luck (issued by a West End firm), dated 1904, where from the birth-date is drawn up a list of days bound to be lucky and others bound to be unlucky ; not only so but it points out which *hours* are lucky, and which are not lucky. Scores of people bought these guides, thereby showing the prevalence of the superstition within recent years.

Some writers have traced the evil influence to the *day* and others to the *person* and the *day* together ;

that is, some days are bad for everybody, other days are bad for some people but possibly good for others.

In *Precepts, etc., left by William Lord Burghley to his Sonne*, we read : " Though I think no day amisse to undertake any good enterprise or businesse in hande, yet have I observed some, and no meane clerks, very cautionarie to forbeare these three Mundayes in the yeare, which I leave to thine owne consideration, either to use or to refuse ; viz., 1. The first Munday in April, which Day *Caine was born, and his brother Abel slaine.*   2. The second Munday in August, which day *Sodome and Gomorrah were destroyed.*   3. The last Munday in December, which day *Judas was born* that betrayed our Saviour Christ."

Quaint, if not humorous reasons are assigned for the existence of evil luck in the book referred to, but in the following from Grafton's *Manual* (1565) there is nothing but sheer dogmatism :—

" The unlucky Days according to the opinion of the Astronomers are noted, which I have extracted as follows :—' January 1, 2, 4, 5, 10, 15, 17, 29, very unlucky.   February 26, 27, 28, unlucky ; 8, 10, 17, very unlucky.   March 16, 17, 20, very unlucky. April 7, 8, 10, 20. unlucky ; 16, 21, very unlucky. May 3, 6, unlucky ; 7, 15, 20, very unlucky.   June 10, 22, unlucky ; 4, 8, very unlucky.   July 15, 21, very unlucky.   August 1, 29, 30, unlucky ; 19, 20, very unlucky.   September 3, 4, 21, 23, unlucky ; 6, 7, very unlucky.   October 4, 16, 24, unlucky ; 6 very unlucky. November 5, 6, 29, 30, unlucky ; 15, 20, very unlucky. December, 15, 22, unlucky ; 6, 7, 9, very unlucky'."

I imagine I hear the reader say " What of Friday ? " Yes, no doubt, Friday has been regarded as unlucky for ages, but surely the fact of the Crucifixion is enough to account for it ? That sailors who have no religion still hold to the habit of refusing to sail, is an item of no importance, for all men are superstitious who have to deal with the great forces of Nature at first hand ; forces on whose will they are almost entirely dependent. In cases where those forces have been brought more under control by steam power vessels, the superstition has decreased in proportion ; a "sailor" on a New York liner is not so troubled about starting from port on a Friday as a sailor of the crew of a barque would be. The barque depends on wind and weather entirely ; the liner goes on, and although delayed by both, is not at their mercy.

John Gibbon prints the following epistle to himself. He was the eccentric author of *Some Memorable Remarques upon the 14th of October.* It is a curious instance of Friday superstition :—"A letter from Sir Winston Churchill, Knight, Father to the Right Hon. John, Lord Churchill. I thank you for your kind present, the observation of the fatality of days. I have made great experience of the truth of it, and have set down Friday as my own lucky day; the day on which I was born, christened, married, and I believe will be the day of my death. The day on which had sundry deliverances (too long to relate) from perils by sea and land, perils by false brethren, perils of law suits, etc. I was knighted (by chance, unexpected by myself) on the same day and have had several good accidents happened to me on that day ; and am so superstitious in the belief of its good omen that I chuse to begin any considerable action (that concerns me) on that day." Friday was a lucky day with Charles Dickens.[1]

As to the extent of the Friday superstition, the following notice from the Scotsman (September 6 1900) will give some indication of its grip on the older people in rural districts :—

" A row of paupers' houses, very neatly designed, had just been erected at Abaracle, Mr Rudd, of Ardnamurchan, having advanced a considerable sum for building purposes to the Parish Council on easy terms. Accommodation is provided for ten persons. A few days ago Mr H. M'Pherson, Inspector of Poor, visited Aberbade in order to superintend the removal of the ten selected female paupers to the new cottages. They all occupied houses which were in a wretched state of disrepair, yet each of them resolutely and peremptorily refused to 'flit.' In vain did the inspector dilate on the increased comfort and conveniences to be enjoyed in the new dwellings. The aged dames were invincibly proof against all argument —nor did threats of compulsion and Sheriff's warrants have any terror for them. At length it was elicited that the disinclination to remove was based simply on superstition. The day of the week happened to be Friday ; and it appears that to change quarters on that particular day constitutes a gross and wanton violation of all the canons governing Highland ' flitting.' On discovering that the perversity manifested by the old women was mainly attributable to conscientious scruples, the inspector at once agreed to humour them, and the removals were postponed until the following day, when they were accomplished

[1] *Credulities past and present* p. 579.

without opposition or delay." And as an instance of
rural superstition on the part of a young girl, I quote
the following from *Notes and Queries* (1900):—

"My wife recently advertised for a new maid in a
local paper. A girl, a native of Devonshire, applied
for the situation and, appearing to be in every way
suitable, she was engaged and asked to come on a
given date. That date happened to be on a Friday,
and the girl positively refused to enter on a new
situation on a Friday. She said she would rather
give up the place. We had to submit, and she came
to my house on a Saturday.—A. J. DAVY, Torquay."

> There are the days of which the careful heed,
> Each human enterprise will, favouring, speed :
> Others there are which intermediate fall,
> Marked with no auspice and unomen'd all.
> And these will some and those will others praise,
> But few are versed in mysteries of days.
> Now as a stepmother the day we find
> Severe, and now as is a mother kind.

In the *Every-Day Book* for 1826, under the date of
Easter Sunday, it is remarked that "the coincidences
by which legendary predictions (those of Nixon and
Mother Shipton are referred to) are sometimes fulfilled,
are often curious. The present year may be said to
witness the accomplishment of one. It has been
said—

> ' When *my Lord* falls in *my Lady's* lap,
> England, beware of some mishap ! '—

meaning thereby, that when the festival of Easter falls
near to Lady-day (the 25th of March), this country is
threatened with some calamity. In the year 1818,
Easter-day happened on the 22d of March, and in the
November of that year Queen Charlotte died. In

1826, Easter-day happening on the 26th of March, distress in the commercial world may be regarded as a fulfilment of this prediction." This prophecy by dates, though more general in character, is somewhat akin to that known as " citation "—of which a curious instance is recorded in Spanish history. Peter and John de Carvajal were, in 1312, condemned to death for murder, on circumstantial evidence; and their sentence was, that they should be thrown from the summit of a rock. Ferdinand IV., then King of Spain, resisted obstinately every attempt made to induce him to grant the pardon of the condemned; who, while on the march to the place of execution, solemnly called on God to witness to their innocence, and appealed to His high tribunal, in presence of which they summoned the King to make his appearance in thirty days. His Majesty laughed to scorn the summons; but nevertheless in a few days he fell sick, and retired to a country residence to divert his mind and recover his health—and shake off the remembrance of the summons, which seems to have taken an irremoveable hold upon him. On the thirtieth day, however, he was much better; and, after showing much mirth and cheerfulness in his conversation with the courtiers, and renewing his ridicule of the delusion that the citation of the Carvajals could have any effect, he retired to rest—and was found dead in bed next morning. Many similar instances of citation to the other world are on record; notable among them, George Wishart's prophecy at the stake, that Cardinal Beaton, who had come to gloat on his dying agony, would soon follow him by a violent death—though the prophecy was probably suggested by the reformer's knowledge of the secret plot against the Cardinal's life. Bacon's judgment of such predictions and coincidences is no doubt, on the whole, a sound one :—" My judgment is, that they ought all to be despised, and ought to serve but for winter talk by the fireside. Though, when I say despised, I mean for belief. That that hath given them grace, and some credit, consisteth in these things : 1st, That men mark when they hit, and never when they miss ; as they do also of dreams. 2d, That probable conjectures and obscure traditions many times turn themselves into prophecies ; while the nature of man, which coveteth divination, thinks it no peril to foretell that which indeed they do but collect. The 3rd and last (which is the great one), is that almost all of them, being infinite in number, have been impostures, and by idle and crafty brains merely contrived and feigned after the event passed. It is, however, also worthy of notice that a genuine and solemn citation may tend to work its own fulfilment in the minds of superstitious men, who by permitting the thing to prey upon their own spirit, enfeeble the powers of life, and perhaps at the critical date arouse thus some latent or dormant disease into deadly action." This philosophy of days lucky and unlucky seems to me to be a necessary and natural outcome of experience in those instances where it is strongly developed. He who has a smooth career, minus great exaltations and great depressions, will never notice a malefic influence on Thursdays which is always absent on Saturdays, nor discover the promise that seems to lie in the virtue of a Wednesday morning. But the man with ups and downs is almost certain to have his theories, and to act upon them, unless he be essentially strong-minded enough to believe that thought is master of every situation. From early ages men have been creatures of fear, and the unlucky day is unfortunately one of the lingering testimonies to that fact.

MARRIAGE SUPERSTITIONS AND CUSTOMS

POPULAR SUPERSTITIONS AND CUSTOMS

(1) THE ENGAGEMENT RING.

Courtship, prior to actual marriage, has been described as a biological preparation for nuptial union, in addition to being a social custom. Some of us would prefer to call it a mental preparation; for the fact that two people of opposite sex are drawn together is in itself some evidence of biological fitness. But the social element concerns us here, and the engagement ring seems to have had an interesting history. As an outward sign, rings have figured prominently in marriage and pre-marriage rites from a very remote antiquity; but an engaged couple in the old English period were accustomed to exchange rings; there was a gift from the man to the woman and the woman to the man; the ring being an 'outward bond of fidelity between the two. Prior to the exchange of rings, it was accounted sufficient if the contracting parties broke a piece of gold or silver (each keeping a half), and drank a glass of wine. This is seen in an old play called " The Vow Breaker " (1636), Act I. Scene I., where Young Bateman and Anne are speaking :—

> "*Ba.* Now, Nan, here's none but thou and I ; thy love
> Emboldens me to speak, and cheerfu ly,
> *Here is a piece of gold ;* 'tis but a little one,
> Yet big enough to try and seale a knot,
> A jugall knot on earth, to which high Heaven
> Now cries Amen : say thou so too, and then
> When eyther of us breakes this sacred bond,
> Let us be made strange spectacles to the world,
> To heaven and earth.
> "*An.* Amen, say I ;
> And let Heaven loth me when I falsifie."

Afterwards, on young Bateman's return from the wars, during whose absence Anne has been induced by her father to marry another person, Anne says, " I am married."

> "*Ba.* I know thou art, to me, my fairest Nan :
> Our vows were made to Heaven, and on earth
> They must be ratifide : in part they are,
> By giving of a pledge, *a piece of gold :*
> Which when we broke, joyntly then we swore,
> Alive or dead, for to enjoy each other,
> And so we will, spight of thy father's frownes."

And afterwards, Act iii. Sc. 1, Anne, seeing the ghost of young Bateman, who had hanged himself for her sake, exclaims :

> " It stares, beckons, *points to the peece oj gold*
> *We brake between us :* looke, looke there, here—there !"

Sometimes a piece of money was broken, a practice referred to in Gays's *What d'ye call It ?*

> " Yet, Justices, permit us, ere we part,
> To break this Ninepence as you've broke our heart."
> " *Filbert* (breaking the ninepence)—As this divides, thus are we torn in twain."
> " *Kitty* (joining the pieces)—And as this meets, thus may we meet again."

The actual interchange of rings is seen in Shakespeare's *Twelfth Night.* The priest, who had been privy to all that had passed, is charged by Olivia to reveal the circumstances, which he does in the following lines :

> " A contract of eternal Bond of Love,
> Confirm'd by mutual joinder of your hands,
> Attested by the holy close of lips,
> Strengthen'd by interchangement of your Rings;
> And all the ceremony of this Compact
> Seal'd in my function, by my testimony."

As to why or when the man refused to wear an engagement ring, there does not appear to be any reliable information. Possibly the wearing of a marriage ring by the woman, and the masculine aversion to visible signs of bondage, may have had something to do with it ; at any rate the cause must be sought in psychological sources rather than in anything purely social.

(2) KISSING THE BRIDE.

The *York Missal* and the *Sarum Manual* both enjoin the nuptial kiss, but it should be given in church. It is expressly mentioned in the following line from the old play of *The Insatiate Countess* by Marston :—

> " The kisse thou gav'st me in the church here take."

In some places it is still customary for the men of the marriage party to kiss the bride in church ; although an increasing respect for the altar prevents the event from taking place immediately the bene- diction is pronounced, as was once the rule ; if done at all, the kissing is half furtively concluded in the vestry or in the home of the bride. Vaughan, in his *Golden Grove* (1608), says that "among the Romans the future couple sent certain pledges one to another which most commonly, they themselves afterwards being present, would confirm with a religious kisse." Kissing is a Caucasian habit; orientals being strangers to it. Lombroso discovers its origin in maternal caresses from which it developed into feelings of trust and reverence.

(3) WEDDING RINGS AND BRIDE CAKE.

If a child were to ask its mother who wore the first wedding ring, and the mother were to pass the question on to the historian of social customs, the historian would have to confess not only that he did not know, but that it would be impossible to assign even an approximate date when such rings became a feature in social life. We know from Juvenal (Satire VI.) that the Romans used such rings; we know that the Greeks used them as far back as we can trace; they are found in Egyptian tombs; they appear to have been part of the customs of the earliest civilisations we can trace. It was this "Heathen" origin of the wedding ring which well nigh caused the abolition of it during the time of the Commonwealth.

The facetious author of Hudibras gives us the following chief reasons why the Puritans wished it to be set aside :—

> "Others were for abolishing
> That tool of matrimony, a ring,
> With which the unsanctify'd bridegroom
> Is marry'd only to a Thumb,
> (As wise as ringing of a pig
> That us'd to break up ground and dig)
> The Bride to nothing but her will,
> That nulls the After-Marriage still."

P. 3, c. ii. 1. 303.

The ring is essentially emblematic, a point which is quaintly stated by Swinburne in his *Treatise of Spousals*. "The first inventor of the ring, as is reported [he cites Alberic de Rosa in suo Dictionar. *v.* Annulus], was one Prometheus. The workman which made it was Tubal-Cain: and Tubal-Cain, by the counsel of our first parent, Adam, gave it unto his Son to this end, that therewith he should espouse a Wife, like as Abraham delivered unto his servants bracelets and earrings of gold. *The form of the Ring being circular, that is round and without end,* importeth thus much, *that their mutual love and hearty affection should roundly flow from the one to the other as in a Circle, and that continually and for ever.*"

History records variations in the use of certain fingers for wearing the ring. The Hereford, York, and Salisbury missals direct the ring to be placed on the thumb first of all; then on the second finger, the third, and afterwards the fourth, "where it is to remain." A writer in the *British Apollo* (1708) answers a question:—"Why is it that the person to be married is enjoyned to put a Ring upon the fourth finger of his spouse's left hand?" It is answered, "There is nothing more in this, than that the custom was handed down to the present age from the practice of our ancestors, who found the left hand more convenient for such ornaments than the right, in that it's ever less employed; for the same reason they chose the fourth finger, which is not only less used than either of the rest, but is more capable of preserving a Ring from bruises, having this one quality peculiar to itself, that it cannot be extended but in company with some other finger, whereas the rest may be singly stretched to their full length and straightness.

"Some of the ancients were of opinion, in this matter, that the ring was so worn because to that finger, and to that only, comes an artery from the heart; but the politer knowledge of our modern anatomists having clearly demonstrated the absurdity of that notion, we are rather inclined to believe the continuance of the custom owing to the reason above mentioned."

Bride-cakes originated with us by adoption from a Roman custom called *confarreation*, where marriage was solemnly concluded in the presence of ten witnesses, a cake of wheat or barley being eaten at the same time. Herrick in his *Hesperides* speaking to the bride says :—

> " While some repeat
> Your praise, and bless you, sprinkling you with wheat."

It is difficult to trace the the changes which mark the history of bride-cakes ; at one period as the bride left the church wheat was thrown upon her head ; in a later period the wheat has disappeared altogether and we have bride-cakes, i.e. a supply of them at a single wedding ; still later we can trace the one cake as we know it to-day in all its elaborateness. The custom of passing slices of cake through the wedding ring has gone out of fashion ; although, we are told, maidens still puts such slices under their pillows and dream of their lovers.

(4) BRIDESMAIDS AND BEST MAN.

Bridesmaids seem to date from Anglo Saxon times, among whom, as Strutt informs us, "the bride was led by a matron, who was called the bride's-woman, followed by a company of young maidens who were called the bride's maids."

In later times it was among the offices of the Bride Maids to lead the bridegroom to church, as it was the duty of the bridegroom's men to conduct the bride thither.

This has not been overlooked in the provincial Poem of " The Collier's Wedding " :—

> " Two lusty lads, well dressed and strong,
> Step'd out to lead the Bride along,
> And two young maids of equal size,
> As soon the Bridegroom's hand surprize."

In these days the bridesmaid's duties are confined solely to the bride, but the whole function, past and present masculine as well as feminine, has its origin in the sympathetic instinct ; although, in the case of groomsmen, there are writers who can trace an origin in the notion of defending the bridegroom against a rival who might carry off the bride. " In Sweden weddings formerly took place under cover of night. Behind the high altar of the ancient church at Husaby in Gothland, a collection of long lances with sockets for torches may yet be seen. These were served out to the groomsmen on such occasions both for defence and illumination." A groomsman was thus a " best-man." He was originally a bride-man—see Beaumont and Fletcher's play *A Wife for a Moneth.*

> " My vertuous maid, this day ile be your bride-man.'

Sometimes he was a bride-knight, and it was his duty to lead the bride to church. The changes which occurred in the course of centuries, whereby the duties of bridesmaids and best man became what they

H

are to-day, are due to the general advance in manners. Marriage customs had many elements of extreme vulgarity in them, particularly on the masculine side ; and the developments of later years on the lines of simplicity and reticence are responsible for the better position in which the modern bridesmaid and best man find themselves.

(5) MAY MARRIAGES.

It is accounted unlucky to be married in May. We seem to have got the superstition from the Romans. Ovid says in his Fasti, lib v. :—

> " Nec viduæ tædis eadem, nec virginis apta
> Tempora. Quæ nupsit, non diuturna fuit.
> Hac quoque de causa (si te proverbia tangunt),
> Mense malas Maio nubere vulgus ait."

But there is evidence of heresy during the long centuries of British history, and specified dates in May are quoted as good for marriages.

In the Roman Calendar, so often quoted, several days are marked as unfit for marriages : " Nuptiæ non fiunt," i.e. " Feb. 11, June 2, Nov. 2, Dec. 1." On the 16th of September, it is noted, " Tobiæ sacrum. Nuptiarum Ceremoniæ a Nuptiis deductæ, videlicet de Ense, de Pisce, de Pompa, et de Pedibus lavandis." On the 24th of January, the Vigil of St Paul's Day, there is this singular restriction, " Viri cum Uxoribus non cubant."

In a most curious old Almanac for the year 1559, " by Lewes Vaughan, made for the merydian of Gloucestre," are noted as follow : " The tymes of Weddinges when it begynneth and endeth." " Jan. 14, Weding begin. Jan. 21, Weddinge goeth out.

April 3, Wedding be. April 29, Wedding goeth out. May 22, Wedding begin." And in another Almanac for 1655, by Andrew Waterman, mariner, we have pointed out to us, in the last page, the following days as "good to marry, or contract a wife (for then women will be fond and loving), viz., January 2, 4, 11, 19, and 21. Feb. 1, 3, 10, 19, 21. March 3, 5, 12, 20, 23. April 2, 4, 12, 20, and 22. May, 2, 4, 12, 20, 23. June 1, 3, 11, 19, 21. July 1, 3, 12, 19, 21, 31. August 2, 11, 18, 20, 30. Sept. 1, 9, 16, 18. 28. Oct. 1, 8, 15, 17, 27, 29. Nov. 5, 11, 13, 22, 25. Dec. 1, 8, 10, 19, 23, 29."

It is to be feared, however, that British women will not listen to the counsels of Mr Waterman. They have decided that May is a bad month to marry in, and they will not forego their opinions. Of course, the superstition itself is sheer nonsense; there is not an atom of evidence to prove that it is different from any other month as being malevolent towards matrimony. The one reason why the superstition has held its course almost unbroken is that women would abstain from marriage eleven months out of the twelve if tradition said the eleven were ill-starred. I have never met a man who did not smile at the notion. But once set a train of superstitious thought agoing as to fate and fortune in marriage, and women will accept it whole-heartedly. Perhaps the number of unhappy marriages is a silent factor in the game.

(6) THROWING THE SHOE.

Throwing the old shoe was not always confined to weddings, though the custom nowadays has come to be associated entirely with the going away of bridal couples. Authorities differ concerning the origin of the practice, as well as of the exact meaning attached to it, but there seems to be a general opinion that it has to do with some very ancient ceremony or rite in connection with the transfer of property— woman being regarded as such among the nations where the custom of such a ceremony is first found. There is also the possibility of its referring to the time when the bridegroom carried off the bride by force, though this seems less likely.

It was in the sense of confirming a sale or exchange that the Jews understood the removal and giving of a shoe or sandal. When the kinsman of Boaz consented to waive his claim upon the parcel of land which Naomi would sell, in favour of Boaz, he "drew off his shoe," for "this was a testimony in Israel."

In a different sense the removal of a shoe marks the winding up of negotiations among the laws and ordinances given in the book of Deuteronomy, where the widow who is refused marriage by her husband's surviving brother, is directed to "come unto him in the presence of the elders, and loose his shoe from off his foot," thus asserting her independence and heaping upon him the blame for failure to comply with the law.

When the Emperor Wladimir proposed marriage to the daughter of Reginald, she refused him with the words:

"I will not take off my shoe to the son of a slave."

In Anglo-Saxon marriages the bride's father delivered her shoe to the bridegroom, who touched her on the head with it in token of his authority.

The idea of luck is the principal thought associated with it always in these later times—especially luck in making journeys. [1]

Ben Johnson wrote—

> "Hurl after me a shoe,
> I'll be merry whatever I'll do,"

and old Heywood says—

> "And home again hitherward quick as a bee,
> Now for good luck, cast an old shoe at me;"

while Tennyson ("Lyrical Monologue") tells us—

> "For this thou shalt from all things seek,
> Marrow of mirth and laughter,
> And wheresoe'er thou move, good luck,
> Shall throw her old shoe after."

Undoubtedly it is the remnant of something which came from the Egyptians or some other ancient nation with which the Jews came in contact, though investigation shows that it was never confined to any one race.

There are some interesting points in regard to the practice which have usually been overlooked in treating the subject, for example, the priests and worshippers at the shrines of of the Roman *Cybele*, the Grecian *Ops*, the Canaanitish *Ashtaroth*, and the Egyptian *Isis*, were compelled to remove their sandals.

The shoes and sandals of the Greeks, Romans, Egyptians, and Jews were ornamented with horns, crescents, and other representations of the moon, while at marriage ceremonies the custom of casting the shoe was, and is now, combined with the throwing of flowers and various kinds of grain. These symbols and offerings seem to indicate the propitiation of a

[1] From *The Scrap Book.*

god, probably the deity who presides over productiveness.

(7) THE DUNMOW FLITCH OF BACON.

The recent revivals in the customs of Dunmow render the study of the subject peculiarly interesting ; for this is an instance where a very old institution sees more vigorous life in the later centuries than it did in the earlier; nothing in the old days can have surpassed the celebrations of the years since 1900. Brand opens his remarks thus :—" A custom formerly prevailed, and has indeed been recently observed at Dunmow, in Essex. of giving a flitch of bacon to any married couple who would swear that neither of them, in a year and a day, either sleeping or waking, repented of their marriage. The singular oath administered to them ran thus :—

> " You shall swear by custom of confession,
> If ever you made nuptial trangresssion,
> Be you either married man or wife,
> If you have brawls or contentious strife ;
> Or otherwise. at bed or at board,
> Offended each other in deed or word :
> Or, since the parish-clerk said Amen,
> You wish'd yourselves unmarried agen,
> Or in a twelvemonth and a day,
> Repented not in thought any way,
> But continued true in thought and desire
> As when you join'd hands in the quire.
> If to these conditions, without all feare,
> Of your own accord you will freely swear,
> A whole gammon of bacon you shall receive,
> And bear it hence with love and good leave ;
> For this is our custom at Dunmow well knowne,
> Though the pleasure be ours, the bacon's your own."

The parties were to take this oath before the Prior and Convent and the whole town, humbly kneeling in the churchyard upon two hard, pointed stones, which are still shown. They were afterwards taken upon men's shoulders, and carried first, about the priory churchyard, and after through the town, with all the friars and brethren, and all the towns-folk, young and old, following them with shouts and acclamations, with their bacon before them."

This will give the reader a good idea of the ceremony, which by one writer is traced to an ancient institution of the Lord Fitzwalter, in the reign of King Henry III., who ordered that "whatever married man did not repent of his marriage, or quarrel with his wife, in a year and a day after it, should go to his priory and demand the bacon, on his swearing to the truth, kneeling on two stones in the churchyard."

After a very chequered history—the Lord of the Manor in 1772 would have nothing to do with the custom, and in 1809, one historian says, it was abolished—the practice of offering the flitch was revived in the later years of the nineteenth century, and has continued since then, not always successfully, or regularly, but nevertheless with sufficient popularity to cause a crowd and a holiday. This is all the more remarkable ; for the custom is essentially vulgar, and is founded on a vulgar estimate of marriage. It passes comprehension how respectable people can go through any public ceremonial to attest their happiness in marriage and to win a flitch of bacon. But why *bacon*, the curious reader will ask? To that question there is no answer available, except the utility of the flitch as a household commodity. The same custom prevailed at Whichenover, and it has been traced in Brittany.

(8) Selling Wives.

Within the last twenty years there have been at least a dozen cases reported in the press of men in a low station in life who have sold their wives, under the impression they could legally do so if all parties were willing. One husband parted with his spouse for eighteen pence and a glass of beer. He was evidently in need of a new system of values, as well as some elementary instruction on the marriage law. But Brand, writing in 1808, remarks :—" A remarkable superstition still prevails among the lowest of our vulgar, that a man may lawfully sell his wife to another, provided he deliver her over with a halter about her neck. It is painful to observe that instances of this occur frequently in our newspapers."

In modern transfers, the scene being the bar of a public-house, the halter is missing, and a few coins take its place. But the origin of the custom can only have originated in methods of marriage without the sanction of priest or civil ceremony ; the result being that, as the man does the marrying himself, he concludes he is the sole contracting party, able at will to dispose of his wife as he thinks fit.

(9) Christening Customs.

The custom of giving children apostle spoons is no longer in vogue, the present-day godfather and godmother usually selecting some article of silver— a mug, accompanied perhaps by a spoon, though not one of the apostle variety. In the old days sponsors would give the whole twelve of apostles' spoons ; those in middling circumstances would give four ;

the poorer people would give one, exhibiting the
figure of any saint in honour of whom the child
received its name. The only origin we can imagine
such a practice to have had, lies in the sense of
dedication, i.e. a giving of the child to a life designed
on Christian lines; and in a sense of benefit or
protection, as symbolised by the presence of the
twelve apostles. But the origin of the well-known
toy with bells and a piece of coral at the end
(generally suspended from the necks of infants to
assist them in cutting their teeth), is with the greatest
probability supposed to lie in the belief that coral
was considered an amulet or defence against " fascination." Pliny supports this view. And Plat, in his
Jewel-House of Art and Nature, says : " Coral is good
to be hanged about children's necks, as well to rub
their gums as to preserve them from the falling sickness ; it hath also some special simpathy with nature,
for the best coral being worn about the neck, will turn
pale and wan if the party that wears it be sick, and
comes to its former colour again as they recover
health" Scott, in his *Discovery of Witchcraft*, remarks :—" The coral preserveth such as bear it from
fascination or bewitching, and in this respect they
are hanged about children's necks. But from whence
that superstition is derived, or who invented the lye,
I know not ; but I see how ready the people are to
give credit thereunto by the multitude of corals that
were employed."

The truth about the coral belongs to the chemist
and not the antiquarian.

DIVINATION AND OMENS

DIVINATION AND OMENS

(1) DREAMS.

George du Maurier, in his *Peter Ibbetson*, has given one of the best descriptions extant of the life of dreams. He says the whole cosmos is in a man's brains, so much at least as a man's brains will hold. And when sleep relaxes the will, and there are no earthly surroundings to distract attention—no duty, pain, or pleasure to compel it—riderless fancy takes the bit in his teeth, and the whole cosmos goes mad, and has its wild will of us. There are the "ineffable false joys"—how well we know them; "the unspeakable false terror and distress"—we know them, too; and they chase each other without rhyme or reason, and play hide and seek across the twilit field, and through the dark recesses of our clouded and imperfect consciousness. No wonder that early man, with sufficient intelligence to remember his dreams, and ponder over them fearfully, was, in his ignorance, persuaded they conveyed serious messages to him, messages in which the more clever men of the group saw an opening for personal ascendancy by devising a system of interpretation, and thus assuming a position of importance and leadership in the tribe. That dreams should occupy so prominent a position in

divination is not at all surprising. Dream life—
indeed sleep life altogether—is still an unsolved problem, and when the coincidences of events as between
dreaming and waking are taken into account, it is
most natural that primitive man and civilised man
should try to turn dreams into a science, and formulate
a skilful list of interpretations. Besides, in all Christian countries there is a solid reason for accepting
information conveyed in dreams, inasmuch as the
sacred narratives in the Bible allege Divine guidance
by this means. We may, of course, have our own
interpretation of such phenomena, but the wide stretch
of centuries covered by these facts is not without
significance, showing as it does the strong and tenaci-
ous grip which dream interpretation had upon the
race. From Jacob's dream to that of Pilate's wife is a
far cry, and yet both Jew and Pagan agreed in the
real importance of the dream as a guide to life and
conduct.

But a distinction was made between the various
kinds of dreams, or rather the better type of mind
attempted to make such a distinction, though seldom
with success. In the Christian and Pagan worlds no
notice was taken of the wild, incoherent, purposeless
dream, except by a class of low magicians who sought
money by exploiting the fears of the fearful. Nevertheless, if one kind of dream came from God, or the
gods, where did the others come from? Here was an
opportunity for the sharks of occultism, and for the
charlatan generally. The dream-book and the diviner
came into being, and they have never yielded to pressure from civil or military authorities. You cannot
stamp out a superstition which has its basis in the

operations of sleep, over which men and women have practically no control. Only a right understanding of the subject can rob the superstitious of their fears aud the credulous of their credulity. To forbid dreaming by Act of Parliament would be a non-sensical procedure; and yet it is just as absurd to attempt to keep people from wondering what is the meaning of their dreams.

If we look carefully for the origin of dream super-stition, we shall find one source in the Pagan tradition of the importance of dreams in conjunction with the high place given to them in the Bible; another source is the long and historical list of remarkable coinci-dences; and a third source is the somewhat humiliat-ing fact that we do not yet know the nature of dreams and sleep.

Take the last point first. Here is a brief account of some experiments regarding the brain and the mysteries of sleep recently made by Professor Wenley of Michigan University, who declares authoritatively that the investigations have destroyed many accepted theories. The accepted theory of sleep has been the lessening of the blood-pressure in the brain.

The experiments showed directly opposite condi-tions. By delicate and most careful measurements, the following results were tabulated :—

'The size or volume of the brain increases when the individual goes to sleep, and decreases when he awakens. On this point it was noted that in some cases the brain became smaller at first, and then in-creased as the sleep became deeper. Very striking was the evidence that the size of the arterial pulse in the brain increases steadily with the increase in the volume—*i.e.*, that the dilating of the arteries after each beat of the heart is more pronounced. This is particularly true when the subject is propped up. As the sleep passes off, the brain volume decreases, but then the blood - pressure increases. These results show that whatever sleep may be caused by, it is not a lessening of the blood-supply to the brain, for there is no such lessening.'

What kind of consciousness, therefore, is dream consciousness? The question remains unanswered.

What impresses most of us in regard to dreams is that, although the fearful experience of the after effects of a lobster salad supper is classified as a dream, there are sober, more sensible, realistic dreams which appear to convey information in reference to the future. Are these messages from extraneous intelligences, or just the chance successes of dreaming moments? It is not easy to say. Unless the reader has had such a dream, he is inclined to be sceptical as to its existence. This scepticism is hardly justified when one considers the mass of evidence submitted by people who have no object in stating untruths.

And even when 25 per cent. is deducted for exaggeration, or faulty memory, there is a residue which chance can hardly account for, without straining the facts of psychology. I propose to reproduce a few cases, making a commencement by recording the dream of a British Consul, as contained in Hutchinson's *Dreams and Their Meanings* :—

"Mr Haggard of the British Consulate, Trieste, Austria, gives the following account of a premonitory dream and its fulfilment :—

' 21st September, 1893.

'A few months ago I had an extraordinary vivid dream, and waking up repeated it to my wife at once. All I dreamt actually occurred about six weeks afterwards. There seems to have been no purpose in the dream, and one cannot help thinking what was the good of it. I dreamt that I was asked to dinner by the German Consul General, and, accepting, was ushered into a large room with trophies of East African arms on shields against the walls. (I have myself been a good deal in East Africa.) After dinner I went to inspect the arms, and amongst them saw a beautifully gold-mounted sword which I pointed out to the French Vice-Consul, who at that moment joined me, as having probably been a present from the Sultan of Zanzibar to my host, the German Consul General. At that moment the Russian Consul came up, too. He pointed out how small was the hilt of the sword, and how impossible in consequence it would be for a European to use the weapon ; and whilst talking, he waved his arm in an excited manner over his head, as if he were wielding the sword, and to illustrate what he was saying. At that moment I woke up, and marvelled so at the vividness of my dream that I woke my wife up, too, and told it to her. About six weeks afterwards my wife and myself were asked to dine with the German Consul General ; and the dream had long been forgotten by us both. We were shown into a large withdrawing-room, which I had never been in before, but which somehow seemed familiar to me. Against the walls were some beautiful trophies of East African arms, among which was a gold-hilted sword, a gift

I

from the Sultan of Zanzibar. To make a long story short, everything happened exactly as I had dreamt.' In a long letter Mrs Haggard confirms her husband's narrative."

Before attempting an interpretation of this occurrence, I should like to bring to the reader's notice Mr Greenwood's theory of mental duality. He says :—

"It is easy to imagine the mind of man dual—its faculties supplied in a double set. Duality seems to be a common law in nature. The brain, which is the mind machine, is itself a dual organ ; and nearly all the difficulty of understanding dreams would disappear if we could believe that our mental faculties are duplex, and that, though the two sets work together, inseparably and indistinguishably, while we live our natural lives in the waking world, they are capable of working apart, the one under the observation of the other, more or less, when all are out of harness by the suspension of the senses in sleep.[1]"

In remarking on this passage Mr H. G. Hutchinson says :—"We give an instance of this kind of dream, which appears to us to be only thoroughly accounted for by the theory of dual personality. The lady who was the dreamer lives in Kensington, and had an office in which she carried on a business in Knightsbridge, the office being about two miles from her house :—'On the night of — I dreamt very distinctly that I saw a crowd, and I heard a voice saying, 'She is quite dead, I've cut her throat. I've cut her throat.' I was very frightened, as it impressed me as being so *real.* I awoke and noted the time, 4 A.M.   The next

[1] Greenwood. *Imagination in Dreams.*

morning at breakfast I told my family, including my
cousin, Miss M. D. When I arrived at my place of
business, I saw a crowd outside the next door house,
and found on enquiry that a man had murdered his
wife by cutting her throat about 4 A.M. in this house.

(Signed) A. W. W.'

'My cousin told me her dream at breakfast on —,
and I remember hearing in the evening that a murder
had taken place in the house next door to my cousin's
office in the early morning.

(Signed) M. D.'

" Miss A. W. W. was worried about her business at
the time ; does it not seem a simple explanation that
her dual personality was haunting her office at the
time, and saw the commotion when the police discovered the crime, and thus conveyed the impression
to her sleeping brain ? [1] "

I am afraid this dual theory is pressed too far
and asked to account for too much. In our
dreams we are the same Egos as in our waking
moments; and we see the same people we know
in daily life, and recognise them ; proving that there
is an exercise of the same memory centres as
in conscious life. The direction in which we are
likely to find the truth is telepathy, although how
even that, as yet, undemonstrated science can see
into the future (as in the consul's dream), passes
our comprehension. Nevertheless, if sleep itself is
still a problem minus a solution, it need not disturb
our equanimity to have a few unsolved items in
the world of dreams. The subject is only referred

[1] Hutchinson, *Dreams and Their Meanings*, p. 186.

to here as an explanation of the tenacity of dream superstitions; for if we knew why we dream a dream several nights in succession, or why we dream of wheat one night, and falling down a precipice the next, we might reasonably expect an enlightened world to treat their dreams humorously — not seriously as too often is their wont.

Dreams are still believed in by a vast number of people as conveying warnings, or news about the events of the future. They do not accept the superstition openly, but secretly : they divine their dreams in the privacy of their rooms with the dream book open before them. One of these books I propose to examine at some length, because it is popular in style, detailed in its rules of interpretation, and evidently a good seller. My copy is marked the third edition : 10,000 copies. I refer of course, to Raphael's *Dream Book*. The author starts out with what he evidently believes is safe ground, namely that dreams are *prophetic* because they have a divine significance, as is proved from the narratives of the Bible. Now it must be admitted that to believers in the Bible, *i.e.* the literal truth, of O. T. biographies especially, this is a fact with considerable weight. If the Deity has guided his people by dreams in one age, why not in another? The question is not altogether illogical, and it explains in great measure the sense of awe which comes upon a man who has had a remarkable and vivid dream about an event in his own career. But this point has been dealt with already, and I hasten on to scrutinise Raphael's method of divination. Here it is :—

EXAMPLE.

Suppose I am desirous of knowing the interpretation of my dream, I proceed to make at random ten rows of ciphers or noughts.   Thus—

Sign 1.

ooooooooooo,	12 ciphers, or even,	o o
ooooooooo,	9 „ odd,	o
ooooooooooooooo,	15 „ „	o
oooooo,	6 „ even,	o o
ooooooooo,	10 „ „	o o

Sign 2.

ooooooooooooo,	14 ciphers or even,	o o
oooooooooo'	11 „ odd,	o
ooooooooooooo,	13 „ „	o
ooooooooooooo,	14 „ even,	o o
ooooooooooo,	12 „ „	o o

Now I put Signs Nos. 1 and 2 together.   Thus—

Index.

o o	o o	= 4 ciphers, or even,	o o
o	o	= 2 „ „	o o
o	o	= 2 „ „	o o
o o	o o	= 4 „ „	o o
o o	o o	= 4 „ „	o o

Having added the ciphers together, they produce what is called the *Index*. With this Index I refer to the Table of Indexes, and find this Sign refers to the Hieroglyphical Emblem of *Aries*. Then I turn to the Interpretations and find *Aries*, which is on page 9, and amongst the Signs I look for those above, viz., and the Interpretation of the Dream is—*An uncommon omen; cares and toils are denoted. A harassing time after this dream. Be very careful.*

Possibly Raphael thought this method of divining was rather irksome at times, so he provided a long list of what might be called snap-shot interpretations, equipped with an alphabetical arrangement to facilitate reference. A sample page will give the reader an idea of the scheme :—

HARVEST.—To dream of harvest, and that you see the reapers at work, and hear the shouts of "Harvest home!" is a most favourable dream. You could not have had a better. It denotes prosperity to the farmer especially, many customers to the tradesmen, a safe and prosperous voyage to the mariner, and lucrative bargains to the merchant.

HAT.—To dream you have a new hat, portends success. To dream you lose your hat, or that it is taken off your head, you have an enemy not far off who will both openly and secretly seek your injury.

HATE.—To dream you hate a person, denotes you will always have a good friend in the time of need.

HAWK.—If you dream you see a hawk, it signifies you are going to begin some new enterprise; if the hawk darts down and takes a chicken, or a bird, you will succeed; but if the little bird attack the hawk, you will meet many difficulties and, perhaps, failure.

HAY.—To dream you cut hay, indicates you will have great influence in society. To dream of raking it, denotes you will be respected by gentry and nobility.

HEART.—To dream your heart is diseased, denotes you have too much blood in your system; should you dream you are affected with palpitation or violent beating of the heart, it denotes great trouble.

HEAT.—To dream of being in a place extremely hot, or if the weather is so hot that the heat affects you, denotes anger, and that some person is preparing to attack you, or give you a good scolding.

HEAVEN.—To dream of heaven, denotes a change of worlds, and that the remnant of your life will be spiritually happy, and your death peaceful.

HEDGES.—To dream of green hedges, is a sign of agreeable circumstances. If you cannot pass on your way for thorny hedges, it denotes that in business you will suffer by competitions, and in love by rivals.

HEDGEHOG.—To dream you see one, denotes you will meet an old friend whom you have not seen for years.

HEIR.—To dream you are an heir to property, signifies you will be left almost penniless by those of your relations who are wealthy. It is not a good dream.

HELL.—This dream forebodes bodily and mental agony, arising from enemies, loss in trade, bereavements, etc.

HEN.—To hear hens cackle in your dream, signifies joy, love.

Of course it is easy to say "bosh," and to declare this interpretation of dreams is a more amusement. It is more than that. Deep down in their hearts many people fear "there is something in it;" and although they never openly acknowledge the fact, they—women especially—shew their curiosity and their superstition by harbouring the dream book and pondering its interpretations. A lively sense of humour is the best antidote. The girl who dreams of a new hat—and many do—and believes it really means success, is a hopeless creature. And the authors and publishers of dream books should have the attention of the Censor.

Considering the 40 millions of people living in these islands, the really remarkable dreams are few in number, that is, remarkable in the prophetic sense; for, granting that a good percentage never become known to the public, the presumption is that only men and women with strong telepathic natures "dream the dream that comes true." Such people are exceedingly scarce, and most of our dreams have origins like that described by Macnish in his *Philosophy of Sleep*:—

" I believe that dreams are uniformly the resuscitation or re-embodiment of thoughts which have formerly, in some shape or other, occupied the mind. They are old ideas revived, either in an entire state, or heterogeneously mingled together. I doubt if it be possible for a person to have, in a dream, any idea whose elements did not, in some form, strike him at a previous period. If these break loose from their connecting chain, and become jumbled together incoherently, as is often the case, they give rise to absurd combinations; but the elements still subsist, and only manifest themselves in a new and unconnected shape. As this is an important point, and one which has never been properly insisted upon, I shall illustrate it by an example :—

' I lately dreamed that I walked upon the banks Of the Great Canal in the neighbourhood of Glasgow. on the side opposite to which I was, and within a

few feet of the water, stood the splendid portico of
the Royal Exchange. A gentleman, whom I knew,
was standing upon one of the steps, and we spoke to
each other. I then lifted a large stone, and poised
it in my hand, when he said that he was certain I
could not throw it to a certain spot which he pointed
out. I made the attempt, and fell short of the mark.
At this moment a well-known friend came up, whom
I knew to excel at *putting* the stone ; but, strange to
say, he had lost both his legs, and walked upon
wooden substitutes. This struck me as exceedingly
curious ; for my impression was that he had only
lost one leg, and had but a single wooden one. At
my desire he took up the stone, and, without difficulty,
threw it beyond the point indicated by the gentleman
upon the opposite side of the canal. The absurdity
of this dream is extremely glaring ; and yet, on
strictly analysing it, I find it to be wholly composed
of ideas, which passed through my mind on the
previous day, assuming a new and ridiculous arrangement. I can compare it to nothing but to cross
readings in the newspapers, or to that well-known
amusement which consists in putting a number of
sentences, each written on a separate piece of paper,
into a hat, shaking the whole, then taking them out
one by one as they come, and seeing what kind of
medley the heterogeneous compound will make when
thus fortuitously put together. For instance, I had,
on the above day, taken a walk to the canal along
with a friend. On returning from it, I pointed out
to him a spot where a new road was forming, and
where, a few days before, one of the workmen had
been overwhelmed by a quantity of rubbish falling

upon him, which fairly chopped off one of his legs, and so much damaged the other that it was feared amputation would be necessary. Near this very spot there is a park, in which, about a month previously, I practised throwing the stone. On passing the Exchange on my way home, I expressed regret at the lowness of its situation, and remarked what a fine effect the portico would have were it placed upon more elevated ground. Such were the previous circumstances, and let us see how they bear upon the dream. In the first place, the canal appeared before me. (2) Its situation is an elevated one. (3) The portico of the Exchange, occurring to my mind as being placed too low, became associated with the elevation of the canal, and I placed it close by on a similar altitude. (4) The gentleman I had been walking with was the same whom, in the dream, I saw standing upon the steps of the portico. (5) Having related to him the story of the man who lost one limb, and had a chance of losing another, this idea brings before me a friend with a brace of wooden legs, who, moreover, appears in connection with putting the stone, as I know him to excel at that exercise. There is only one other element in the dream which the preceding events will not account for, and that is, the surprise at the individual referred to having more than one wooden leg. But why should he have even one, seeing that in reality he is limbed like other people? This, also, I can account for. Some years ago, he slightly injured his knee while leaping a ditch, and I remember jocularly advising him to get it cut off. I am particular in illustrating this point with regard to dreams, for I hold that, if it were possible to analyse them all, they would invariably be found to stand in the same relation to the waking state as the above specimen. The more diversified and incongruous the character of the dream, and the more remote from the period of its occurrence the circumstances which suggest it, the more difficult does its analysis become ; and, in point of fact, this process may be impossible, so totally are the elements of the dream often dissevered from their original source, and so ludicrously huddled together."

The serious side of dream superstitions is the same as the serious side of palmistry : an interpretation which points to disaster may induce the subject voluntarily to end his life. Most dreams, like the one just outlined, are capable of reconstruction from purely natural elements in our own experiences.

(2) WITCHCRAFT.

It is no part of our present purpose to adjudicate on the rights and wrongs of witchcraft—with which we associate wizardry—rather is it our object to trace the fact of its existence, real or alleged, back to the earliest records of history. We may, too, look at the few remaining instances in modern times of what was once a great source of fear, evil, and cruelty.

Chaldean magic is, so far as expert investigation can tell, the real source of that witchcraft which for centuries disturbed the peace of rural populations in Europe, and engaged the angry attentions of priest and layman alike. It should not be presumed that the magic of any nation, living or dead, is a thing to be laughed out of court ; a sort of jugglery that could be learned like the skill of the conqueror.   It was something more than that.   True we cannot say exactly what it was, or is, for the practices of modern savage tribes have an unknown element of psychic power in them, a fact which is attested by reliable travellers and authorities.   Thus in the Malay Peninsula to-day there are black magicians, and their doings are not at all relished by the white man whose treatment of them may have been lacking in justice. So, in the earliest ages, we find the same kind of arts practised, followed by the same results, that is, if we can rely on the testimony of those who have recorded them.   In Egypt, in Persia, in Greece, in India, and the East generally, there was a definite place assigned to magic ; and magic, generically, was the use of an unseen and powerful agency for the purpose of creating confusion, bestowing evil, taking revenge, and doing all the works of the old time " Devil." For this reason witchcraft and black magic have a strong family relationship, and we can only conclude that since the arts they used are in many cases identical, the later cult was a direct descendant of the earlier.   That a good deal was lost in transit is natural, and this would account for the feebler displays of " power " by women of the middle English period as contrasted with the " success " of the witch of Endor.   Slowly the belief in witches died a natural death, until now, in the twentieth century, it is hardly possible to find a single man or woman who does not think the whole persecutions of the past were founded on ignorance, religious intolerance, and political spite.   The accepted explanation of such phenomena as are considered genuine is that of hypnotism, especially in the case of sympathetic witchcraft, where a witch makes an image of her enemy and pierces it with pins, or melts it before the fire. But this explanation hardly covers the details of the best authenticated reports, and we have either to disbelieve in these reports or fall back upon hypnotism and suggestion. Probably the wisest attitude is that of the agnostic, who, not knowing the real facts, and being unable to get at them, is in no hurry to propound a theory for uncertain phenomena.

But witchcraft and wizardry are not dead entirely. In a London Journal, dated January 9, 1909, I find the following narrative which, on enquiry, proved to be a serious contribution from an English traveller. The evil eye is said to have a dread terror for the more ignorant Erse population, but the story here told is, as will be seen, on true witchcraft lines. " Some months ago I was on a visit to some friends in the south of Ireland, and one morning when seated at breakfast a servant rushed into the room, screaming hysterically that the dairymaid has just found pishogue upon the dairy floor. Pishogue is a white, yellowish fungus made at the dead of night, after a solemn incantation of the devil, according to a secret rite which has been handed down from generation to generation. My host, a ' big ' landlord, sprang to his feet and, followed by his wife and myself, ran hastily out of the house into the trim, cool dairy where, upon the posts of the door, I saw the daubs of pishogue. My host knocked it off quickly with a stick, and then, turning angrily to the weeping dairy maid told her it was nothing at all. But the next minute he informed me under his breath that he might expect bad luck with his dairy, as it was indeed the cursed pishogue. That very evening when his twenty splendid milch cows were driven into their stalls to be milked, a cry of consternation went up from the lips of the milkers; they were absolutely dry; and for months they remained so, while a tenant who lived close to the demesne, an absolutely drunken, impecunious, rascal, was noticed to give up his weekly attendance at Mass, in spite of which irreligious conduct his miserable dairy stock suddenly took the appearance of healthy, well-fed cattle, and every one knew he was the man who had put pishogue upon his master and robbed him of his good. It is a well-known fact that a dairy woman will go to churn as usual, when, to her terror, she will find pishogue daubed upon it. Let her churn for hours, she will make no butter. The usual remedy resorted to by terrified people is to get Mass said in their homes, and the places, cattle, or crops blessed on which the curse has fallen. But that often fails to bring back the good."

Now I cannot say this story, although told circumstantially, is convincing. It is one of those cases which need to be seen, in every stage of development, before one can believe. But it is interesting as a twentieth century tale of wizards and witches, for the midnight rite is conducted by a group of men and women crouching over a smouldering fire. Here is the tale of an old-fashioned witch—of the white variety—reported in the *Diss Express* of December 16, 1893 :—

" The Suffolk Coroner (Mr Charton) on Tuesday held an inquest at the Green Man Inn, Mendlesham, touching the death of a child, named Maggie Alberta

Wade, daughter of Henry Wade, an agricultural labourer. The first witness called was the mother, Elizabeth Wade, who stated that last Friday the deceased pulled a cup of boiling soup over herself and was badly scalded. She did not send for a doctor, but at once sent for an old woman living in the neighbourhood, whose name is Brundish, who, according to witness, is possessed of supernatural powers in the cure of burns and scalds. The old woman came at once, and said some strange words over the child, and passed her hands across the injured parts. Witness, under these circumstances, did not consider the attendance of a medical man necessary, but notwithstanding the woman's incantation, the child died in 40 hours. Witness persisted in expressing her belief in the old woman's power, and said she really was a witch. The female referred to declined to reveal the words spoken, as she said she would lose her power. Other witnesses professed their faith in the professions of the old woman. Eventually, after the Coroner had commented on the superstition exhibited, medical evidence was given to the effect that the child's life could not have been saved."

No action seems to have been taken against the witch in this case, but in the case of malevolent witches the cruelty of the punishment was so severe that we cannot wonder at the total disappearance of black witchcraft in this country. In *The Gentleman's Magazine* for 1751 there is the following entry :—At Tring, in Hertfordshire, one B——d——d, a publican, giving out that he was bewitched by one Osborne and his wife, harmless people above 70, had it cried at several market-towns that they were to be tried by ducking this day, which occasioned a vast concourse. The parish officers having removed the old couple from the workhouse into the church for security, the mob, missing them, broke the the workhouse windows, pulled down the pales, and demolished part of the house; and, seizing the Governor, threatened to drown him and fire the town, having straw in their hands for the purpose. The poor wretches were at length, for public safety, delivered up, stripped stark naked by the mob, their thumbs tied to their toes, then dragged two miles, and thrown into a muddy stream; after much ducking and ill-usage, the old woman was thrown quite naked on the bank, almost choked with mud, and expired in a few minutes, being kicked and beat with sticks, even after she was dead; and the man lies dangerously ill of his bruises. To add to the barbarity, they put the dead witch (as they called her) in bed with her husband, and tied them together. The Coroner's inquest have since brought in their verdict, *wilful murder*, against Thomas Mason, Wm. Myatt, Rich. Grice, Rich. Wadley, James Proudham, John Sprouting, John May, Adam Curling, Francis Meadows, and twenty others, names unknown. The poor man is likewise dead of the cruel treatment he received."

Whenever the modern palmist or fortune-teller comes into contact with the police, the greatest punishment consists of a heavy fine; but in the olden times the magician, wizard, or witch was open to the fury of the mob, as is seen in the case of Tring. Lord Bacon's quaint philosophising as to the origin of witchcraft wonders is worth reproducing :—" Men may not too rashly believe the confession of Witches, nor yet the evidence against them : for the Witches themselves are imaginative, and believe oftentimes they do that which they do not ; and people are credulous in that point, and ready to impute accidents and natural operations to Witchcraft. It is worthy the observing, that, both in ancient and late times (as in the Thessalian witches, and the meetings of Witches that have been recorded by so many late confessions), the great wonders which they tell, of carrying in the air, transforming themselves into other bodies, etc., are still reported to be wrought, not by incantations or ceremonies, but by ointments and anointing themselves all over. This may justly move a man to think that these fables are the effects of imagination ; for it is certain that ointments do all (if they be laid on anything thick), by stopping of the pores, shut in the vapours, and send them to the head extremely."

Reviewing the whole matter, one may conclude that whatever indisputable wonders exist in the history of witchcraft were due to black magic, which is the use of an unknown mental force for the accomplishment of an evil end ; or, if we are unable to accept that hypothesis, we are thrown back on a species of hypnotism. In either case we cannot flatter ourselves on the extent of our knowledge, or the authenticity of our " facts."

(3) DIVINATION BY BOOKS.

In Pagan days the curious would endeavour to peer into the future by opening the pages of Homer or Virgil, and noting the lines covered by the thumb

K

the instant the book was opened. They were read
with a view to casting some light on the problem
which occasioned the consultation. King Charles I.
adopted this method of learning his fate. According
to one account — that of Aubrey — "the King, in
December, 1648, being in great trouble, and prisoner
at Carisbrooke, or to be brought to London to his
tryal, Charles, Prince of Wales, being then at Paris,
and in profound sorrow for his father, Mr Abraham
Cowley went to wayte on him. His Highness asked
him whether he would play at cards to divert his sad
thoughts. Mr Cowley replied he did not care to play
at cards, but if His Highness pleased they would use
Sortes Virgilianæ—(Mr Cowley always had a Virgil
in his pocket)—the Prince liked the proposal, and
pricked a pin in the fourth book of the Æneid," &c.
" The Prince understood not Latin well, and desired
Mr Cowley to translate the verses, which he did
admirably well." The lines were :

> " But vex'd with rebels and a stubborn race,
> His country banish'd, and his son's embrace,
> Some foreign Prince for fruitless succours try,
> And see his friends ingloriously die :
> Nor, when he shall to faithless terms submit,
> His throne enjoy, nor comfortable light,
> But, immature, a shameful death receiye,
> And in the ground th' unbury'd body leave."

They were not at all inapt, and it is easy tr :ee
how a few coincidences of this kind set up a " law "
and establish a cult. Even Christians are not free from
this method of seeking Divine guidance. A man in
great distress will decide to open the Bible, and be
guided by the first words his eyes light upon, thereby
imitating a devout practice dating back to the first

formation of the Scriptures. If the words should be,
" Be still, and know that I am God," he will resolve to
do nothing but wait ; and yet sometimes the words
have been, " Saddle me the ass," or " There is death
in the pot." The result is just like the probabilities
of any other event containing the same possibilities,
and at bottom differs in nowise from the latest Monte
Carlo system.

The origin of the practice is to be found in the
respect and veneration for certain books arising out of
their wisdom and reputation.

(4) DIVINING ROD (DOWSING ROD).

It is curious to read old authors, quite superstitious
in some directions, who suggest the use of a forked
hazel twig to find springs of water is " a vulgar
notion " ; for in modern times there has been not only
a revival of the divining rod for this purpose, but
dowsers, or water finders, are in regular employment.
So recently as 1882 there was a correspondence in
The Times on this subject. Mr E. Vaughan Jenkins
of Westbury and Mendip, Wells, Somerset, wrote as
follows :—" You may possibly like to hear of my
experiences as to the divining rod. In July, 1876,
that very hot summer, the old well under my house
became fouled, and the water unfit to drink, so I
decided on sinking another well, about one hundred
yards from my house, if I were advised that water
could be found there. The field is perfectly dry, and
there is no appearance of water anywhere near where
I wished to sink. I sent for a labouring man in the
village who could 'work the twig,' as the divining
rod is called here, and he came and cut a blackthorn

twig out of my hedge, and proceeded around the field, and at one spot the twig became so violently affected that it flew out of his hands ; he could not hold it.   I may here observe that the village churchyard adjoins my field, and it was of consequence to me to know whether the spring went through or near the churchyard.   So I asked the man to tell me which way the spring ran (of course under the ground), and he proceeded to follow up the spring, and found that it did not go near the churchyard.   Having some doubts as to this man, about a month after I heard of another man, living seven miles off, who, I had been told, could ' work the twig.'   I sent for him, and he was quite unaware the first man had tried for water ; and, to my astonishment, when he came near the spot indicated by the first man, he could not hold the twig, it was so much affected.   I then asked him to tell me the course of the underground spring, and he went as near as possible to the first man—from about S.W. to N.E.   I thereupon decided to sink a well, the last man assuring me that water was not very far down.   At thirty-nine feet the well-sinker came upon a spring of most beautiful water, and there is in the well about thirty feet of water in the summer, and in the winter it is nearly full." [1]   Such narratives as this can be duplicated from literature of more recent date, and Mr Beaven, in his *Tales of the Divining Rod*, has given the whole subject of rod divination a thoroughgoing and up-to-date analysis. [2]

But why a *rod*?   Why not divine without one?

---

[1] Quoted in *Popular Superstitions*, by G. L. Gomme, p. 317.

[2] Professor W. F. Barrett and Sir Oliver Lodge have made satisfactory tests with dowsers.

The answer of history is that from Babylonian times, probably long before that, the rod was known to have some strange and unaccountable power when held in the hands of mesmeric operators ; it was used, not very successfully, to discover ore bodies ; it figures in all kinds of divination practices, as we can see from the pages of the Old Testament. Here, then, is a so-called superstition which bids fair to become in one specified direction an acknowledged fact. As yet it is purely unscientific ; nobody seems to know why the twig held in the hand becomes agitated when near a spring, but of the fact itself doubt diminishes every year that passes.

(5) PALMISTRY.

Palmistry is said to have been introduced into this country by gipsies in the 16th century.   Mason in his *Anatomie of Sorcery* (1612) speaks of " vaine and frivolous devices of which sort we have an infinite number also used among us, as namely in Palmistry, where men's fortunes are told by looking on the palms of the hande."   From this it would appear that the " science " did not make its advent with much éclat, and Newton, writing nearly a hundred years later, shows that its associations were not of the best.   In his *Tryall of a Man's Owne Selfe* he enquires, "whether the Governors of the Commonwealth have suffered *Palmesters*, fortune-tellers, stage-players, sawce-boxes, enterluders, puppit-players, loyterers, vagabonds, land-leapers, and such like cozening make-shifts, to practise their cogging tricks and rogish trades within the circuite of his authoritie, and to deceive the simple people with their vile forgerie and palterie."   By "governors of the commonwealth" here, it should seem, he means justices of the peace. A very apposite group of questions for a modern J.P. Dr. Ferrand, writing about 1640, in *Love's Melancholy*, tells us that "this act of Chiromancy hath been so strangely infected with superstition, deceit, cheating, and (if durst say so) with magic also, that the canonists, and of late years Pope Sixtus Quintus, have been constrained utterly to condemn it. So that now no man professeth publickely this cheating art, but theeves, rogues, and beggarly rascals; which are now every where knowne by the name of Bohemians, Egyptians, and Caramaras; and first came into these parts of Europe about the year 1417, as G. Dupreau, Albertus Krantz, and Polydore Vergil report."

We are now in possession of hints respecting the history of palmistry, which take us back to 1417. In what direction shall we look for further light, and how far back can we go? We shall, as in the case of astrology, have to look Eastwards and Southwards: to Egypt, to Mesopotamia, to India, and China. And in those countries we shall find that reading palms is as old as the hills; nobody can tell us when it began, for its rules, its findings, its mysteries, have been handed down from one generation to another. It is an attempt to divine the happenings of the future, and since that future is to man a matter of the keenest possible interest, there is every reason to believe palmistry is contemporaneous with the first dawning of reasoning curiosity. And it persists to-day in spite of prosecutions and imprisonments. Men and women still treat it seriously, or semi-seriously; they will readily spend 5s to have their "lines" read ; and they will buy the literature of the subject and ponder over it.   This literature is rather flimsy in character, but there have been nearly a dozen somewhat large and ambitious volumes since the year 1897.   One of these—Benham's *Laws of Scientific Hand Reading* attempts to take up an independent standpoint with some measure of success.   But just as the astrologer can give no adequate reason why the planets should influence us, and why a transit of Venus or any particular aspect of the heavens spells good or ill, so the palmist can offer no appropriate explanation why a life that is only half spent can imprint the number of its years in a semi-circle round the ball of the thumb. As a social recreation, palmistry is both successful and funny ; as a science, it is delusive—sometimes dangerous.

(6) ASTROLOGY.

Astrology is probably the oldest pseudo-science in the world ; it is one of the first guesses at the riddle of existence that took on mathematical and scientific shape.   To be just, I shall have to admit that throughout the ages it has been developed somewhat on the lines of observation and experiment—lines to which no man of science can take exception.   The time of the birth of children has been taken and the state of the heavens noted ; any serious illness was observed, and the position of the planets at the time was written down ; marriage, financial disaster, loss of parents, and all the ups and downs of mortal existence were carefully compared with the signs above.   These observations were then compared with those of preceding astrologers, the result being we have a huge literature about the occult heavens, and no age has been minus its astrologer. It is but fair to admit, further, that astrology in the hands of its best exponents is not lacking in dignity. If our lives are to be governed by anything in Nature, we prefer to have them governed by the starry host ; in fact, a few of us would prefer the planets to some of the majorities which obtain in the House of Commons. But, judged scientifically, astrology must be regarded as a superstition, because its character readings are too vague, and its "directions" too obscure ; it was a much vaunted "science" long before the discovery of Uranus and Neptune—days when the Moon even was called a planet. In the thousands of years of its existence, it has not appealed successfully to the trained mind skilled in Nature knowledge, and although a few great names are included in its list, from Isaac Newton to the late Dr. Richard Garnet of the British Museum, together with Dean Farrar, the bulk of learned mankind has never looked upon the casting of horoscopes as more than a social amusement.

"Then why," asks some devotee," does it persist ? Why does it not die, like many other so-called superstitions ? Is not this persistency a testimony to its truth ?" No, it is a testimony to a fact in human nature ; that is, we want to know what the future has in store for us. Astrology professes to tell us, hence when the credulous (and a few who are not credulous) see an offer in the paper to the effect that for one shilling "you can know your future," there is no need to be surprised at the persistency of a superstition. In order to meet the demand for information respect-

ing events to come, the smaller fry of the astrological world are prepared to pronounce on the details of business ; they will even cater for the Stock Exchange speculator, and draw up the horoscope of a Limited Company, whose shares are quoted in the official list. This careful working out of details is no new thing : the astrologer simply adapts himself to changing conditions. Werenfels in his *Dissertation upon Superstition* thus describes a superstitious man :—
" He will be more afraid of the Constellation-fires than the flame of his next neighbour's house. He will not open a vein till he has asked leave of the planets. He will avoid the sea whenever Mars is in the middle of Heaven, lest that warrior god should stir up pirates against him. In Taurus he will plant his trees, that this sign, which the astrologers are pleased to call fix'd, may fasten them deeper in the earth. He will make use of no herbs but such as are gathered in the planetary hour. Against any sort of misfortune he will arm himself with a ring, to which he has fixed the benevolent aspect of the stars, and the lucky hour that was just at the instant of flying away, but which, by a wonderful nimbleness, he has seized and detained."

There are modern analogies to this picture, not only in the East, but in the West. London women especially are easily vulnerable—I mean, of course, the few who have little else to do and think about. They will not take a journey without consulting their " directions " for the year ; they have the right times and seasons for paying calls, and would not " hunt," no, not for the world, if the planets were in bad aspect.

Human curiosity, the keen desire to peer into the

future, must have manifested itself in the earliest dawning of the human mind; and the hearts of men being the same fundamentally in all ages, the same wish for a glimpse ahead manifests itself to-day. Writers have sought industriously for the origin of astrology, but have never been successful, except in the general sense of tracing the cult of the stars to the borders of the prehistoric. In some form or other it is as old as the race.

(7) CRYSTAL GAZING.

A London publisher of books on mental science and occultism advertises a crystal gazing outfit in the following terms :—

CRYSTAL GAZING OUTFIT, A COMPLETE.—This outfit consists of a perfectly cut and polished 2 in. transparent solid crystalline sphere ; a beautifully turned and polished ebony pedestal, and a circular full of instructions and suggestions. 3s 6d net, boxed and post free 3s 9d, foreign postage 1s extra.

By Crystal Gazing is meant the practice of gazing steadily into the limpid depths of a solid, crystalline sphere, for the purpose of seeing visions therein. Many people can thus see "pictures" of great personal interest and importance. The visions seem to be in the crystal itself, but the scientific explanation is that the peculiar effect upon the optic nerve provokes to activity some latent clairvoyant function of the brain, which may have been extensively used by primeval man.

It is well known among psychic investigators that Crystal Gazers often see visions of a clairvoyant or telepathic nature. For instance, the experimenter might see, in his Crystal, a moving picture representing a distant friend in a most exciting situation. Subsequent inquiry, by correspondence, has been known to show that the vision correctly portrayed the actual event at the identical time it took place. This is a mere suggestion of the

many interesting phenomena developed by Crystal Gazing.
It is a harmless, amusing pastime.
As a matter of fact, the Crystal is a beautiful ornament,
and is worth its price as a paper weight. This is the
cheapest and best Crystal Gazing offer ever made.

This is business and exposition combined. No
doubt the publisher knows very well that he is
on right and safe lines, for has not Mr Andrew Lang
himself written most interestingly about "scrying," as
crystal gazing is called, and did he not record
the following incident ? —

"I had given a glass ball to a young lady, Miss
Baillie, who had scarcely any success with it. She
lent it to Miss Leslie, who saw a large, square,
old-fashioned, red sofa, covered with muslin (which
she afterward found in the next country-house she
visited). Miss Baillie's brother, a young athlete,
laughed at these experiments, took the ball into
his study, and came back looking 'gey gash.' He
admitted that he had seen a vision—somebody he
knew, under a lamp. He said he would discover
during the week whether he saw right or not. This
was at 5.30 on a Sunday afternoon. On Tuesday Mr
Baillie was at a dance in a town 40 miles from
his house, and met a Miss Preston. 'On Sunday,'
he said, "about half-past five, you were sitting under
a standard lamp, in a dress I never saw you wear,
a blue blouse with lace over the shoulders, pouring
out tea for a man in blue serge, whose back was
towards me, so that I only saw the tip of his
moustache.' "Why, the blinds must have been up,'
said Miss Preston. 'I was at Dulby,' said Mr Baillie,
and he undeniably was."

Yes, when Mr Andrew Lang certifies the reality of crystal gazing, it is justified in the eyes of many people, and instead of being a modern credulity, it becomes a modern—well, not exactly a modern science—it is not far enough advanced for that—but it assumes a rational atmosphere which nothing else could give it. Hence the popularity of the crystal and the cult of the "gaze." But is there anything in it after all? Certainly there is; it is, in fact, a sub-department of hypnotism, the facts of which few readers will care to question. But as yet not many would-be "scryers" are as successful as their efforts are presevering.

French criticism has been somewhat severe.

"Dr Pierre Janet, one of Charcot's coadjutors at the Saltpetrière, said in a lecture at the University of Lyons, in France, that very few persons really 'see things' in crystals, the estimate of 20 per cent. put forward by the Society for Psychical Research being, in his opinion, exaggerated. He has found, too, that this faculty is seldom met with among persons in sound bodily and mental health, it being, in fact, a neurosis, or disease of the nerves, to which only abnormally nervous or hysterical persons are subject. The state induced by prolonged gazing at a faintly luminous object is, on the same authority, a kind of incomplete hypnotism in which hallucinations occur which are in every way deceptions of the senses. But these hallucinations have for their subjects only those things which are within the conscious or unconscious memory of the gazer, and one is just as little likely to gain from them any hint of facts lying within the gazer's knowledge, as to learn the future from the stammerings of anybody drunk. Thus in one case collected by the Psychical Research Society, where the speculatrix—to use the old-fashioned word for such seers—saw in the crystal a newspaper announcing the death of a friend, which afterward turned out to have actually happened, Dr Janet is able to show that there was in the room a real newspaper with the announcement in question, the inference being that the speculatrix had read and mentally noted it without consciously grasping its significance. This experienee might be paralleled by one from Binet, where a student on his way to an examination in Botany, saw to his astonishment the words *Verbascum thapsus* written on the swing door of a well known restaurant. A second examination transformed the two words into the simple ' bouillon,' and it was only then that he remembered that *Verbascum thapsus* was the Linnæan name of the herb called by French peasants *bouillon blanc.*" [1]

This kind of criticism cannot be ignored, but it savours of the dogmatic attitude taken up by Dr Crichton Browne (in his *Dreamy Mental States*) towards anything and everything which cannot be justified by the present knowledge embodied in medical science. There is surely a better way of dealing with phenomena that are capable of scientific verification. If it be possible to see persons and things at a distance by looking into a glass of water, a round piece of glass, or other object with a shining surface, then the laws of the scientific method, i.e. observation and experiment, can be employed with sufficient exactitude to determine the truth or error of

[1] From *The Encyclo of Superstitions*,

the claims put forward. Research Societies have
already made the attempt, but the results have not
been all that one could wish. Spasmodic efforts have
not the same value as systematic and repeated investigation at the hands of a number of trained men.

Crystal gazing presents one of a batch of interesting
phenomena, which began to assert themselves in the
early history of man ; were for ages classed as
credible facts, then branded as unholy superstitions ;
lastly, they display a tendency to return to the first
position, with the added confirmation which comes
from science. Thus the origin of the practice is easily
found. Early in the history of man some member of
the race, more gifted than his fellows in the sense of
being more susceptible to finer influences, saw, or
imagined he saw, visions in the shining pool. He
communicated these to his comrades, and some of
them confirmed the fact by seeing the visions also.
Then the cult, began and developed into divination
as we see it in Pagan rites, and even in the Old
Testament. The crystal itself is not a necessity. As
Mr Lang says, people stared into a "crystal ball; a
cup; a mirror; a blot of ink (Egypt and India); a
drop of blood (the Maoris of New Zealand) ; a bowl
of water (American Indians) ; a pond (Roman and
African) ; water in a glass bowl (Fez) ; or almost
any polished surface." Unlike many superstitions of
the past this, along with others of occult character,
holds the fort against all comers ; sometimes the
enemy makes a breach in the walls and otherwise
demolishes the citadel, but the repairs are as rapidly
executed, and "scrying"—partly a serious study and
partly a social pastime—lives on confident in its

future success. It will be interesting to see what will happen during the next twenty-five years, but unless the subject is severely analysed and experimented upon it will, at the end of that time, be where it is to-day ; a number of people in all grades of society will be ardent devotees, and a still greater number will call them " a credulous crowd," worse than the superstitious nations of the past.

(8) COLOUR SUPERSTITIONS.

Few, if any, of the subjects dealt with in this book offer more items of interest for the student than this which has relation to the importance of colour.   There has always been a superstitious use of colour in connection with astrology, the planets not only having a *number*, but a favourite *hue*, which those people whose date of birth falls within the sphere of the planet should be careful to cultivate.   Hence the readiness of the West End occultist to furnish your number and colour as determined by your name.   No doubt, from this point of view, the rationale of personal colour, sanctioned by fate or fortune, is just as sound or unsound as anything else in astrological lore. But the point of interest lies here : modern medical research has proved the importance of colour in a curative sense.   Your native colour may be pink, and mine may be green, according to the lore of antiquity ; it does not matter much one way or the other.   But it matters a great deal whether we lie in a room of sickness with a red wall paper or a blue one, if there really be a traceable influence of colour on mental conditions.

Now is there such an influence? I think a fairly good case can be made out that there is. Take some of the lowest forms of life—infusoria, for example. Downes and Burns in *Light and Colour* have noticed that infusorial life develops faster under the influence of red and yellow light. Seeds germinate most rapidly under violet and blue rays, and the hatching of silk worms is greatly facilitated by placing the eggs under violet glass. It has been observed also that flies and other insects do not flourish, or are killed outright, by the light which comes through blue glass or blue gauze. When we come to the insect world, the very existence of flowers, with their almost endless gradations of colour and tint, must be taken as a reasonably clear demonstration that colour has some influence upon the feelings of flower-haunting butterflies, bees, and beetles, though even these feelings may be merely those of preference or indifference. Colour was of the highest significance to primitive man; it is to man as we know him to-day. Dr. Ponza, director of the lunatic asylum at Alessandria, Piedmont, cured many of his insane patients by confining them in rooms, the glass and walls of which were of some uniform colour, such as red, or blue, or violet. One taciturn melancholic became gay and talkative after a sojourn of three hours in a red chamber. Others, after having stayed in these coloured rooms for a time, shewed other equally great changes for the better in their mental condition.[1] Chromotherapy is still a science hardly in its infancy, but, when it has received more

[1] See an article in the *Arena* (1898) on *The Relation of Colour to the Emotions*, by Dr Harold Wilson.

attention than it has had up to the present, we may
expect some interesting developments.

Now this is as far as we can go in matters relating
to colour, at least with confidence. It is impossible
to draw up a list of colours representing intellectual
and moral qualities on a foundation of exact science.
A list of dogmatic statements is the easiest thing in
the world to produce, and a popular author has
done it in his *Colour as a Curative Agent.* Thus
on p. 35 I read the following :—

> " Red—Love, affection, or lust.
> Scarlet—Emotion, anger.
> Deep Crimson—Animality.
> Bright Red—Courage or confidence.
> Dull Orange—Less understanding.
> Brownish Orange—Worldly wisdom.
> Light Yellow—Common sense."

and so forth.

In vain do we look for the basis of this ethics of
colour; it cannot be found. We do not deny that
in the Bible sin is scarlet, and that Mephistopheles
usually appears in scarlet ; one could from the pages
of literature almost justify the list we have quoted
from a popular writer.   But we want more than that.
Even though Fox and Gould affirm yellow and gold
correspond to the intellectual, green to the utilitarian,
red to the sensual, and blue to the spiritual, moral,
or religious nature of man,[1] we require the whole
phenomena to be treated according to the scientific
method before we can accept the *ipse dixit* of any
writer.   There *may* be a colour belonging to us as

[1] *American Journal of Ophthalmology,* vol. iii. p. 251.

individuals; the month in which we were born and
the planet that was in the ascendant at the time
may have conferred it on us; each planet *may* denote
a colour; but of these dogmas and many others
nobody seems to know anything that can be dignified
with the name of knowledge. The fact is they are
rank superstitions.

(9) NUMBERS.

The fortune or fatality contained in numbers, *as
numbers*, seems to date back to the time of
Pythagoras, if not earlier. Jones in his *Credulities
Past* and *Present* has gathered together a vast
amount of historical information which it is no
part of my business to reproduce; it is sufficient
to note that in every age and clime numbers have
formed a part of magical and non-magical ceremonial.
Even to-day the clairvoyant who practises in
London will ask her visitor on what day of the
month he was born, and in what year; then, making
a rapid mental calculation, will inform him whether
the coming year will be good for him, financially,
or whether he is likely to experience sickness and
domestic disquiet. Whatever rules she may follow
in making such calculations have been handed
down to her from the past, so that modern fortune
telling in this particular is no different from the
astrology and sooth-saying of the time of Moses.
Another curious development is seen in a book,
published a few years ago, called *The Mysteries of
Sound and Number*, by Habeeb Ahmad. It claims
that every letter means a number; so that, if you
will take the trouble to arithmetise your own name,
you know what your nnmber is and can act accord-

ingly. How *accordingly* ? Because the planets
have numbers—the sun is No. 1—and as they exert
a favourable influence every few minutes in turn
throughout the day, you have only to act when
your number and the right planet correspond, to
succeed in anything you undertake. Mr Ahmad
applies his logic to horse racing, and has drawn up
a list of examples from past races to show how
true his theory is. Of course horses have names
and he claims they are not given them by chance,
but according to an occult law, just as is the case
with human beings. A new system of horse racing,
where the bookmaker will be "done" every time,
should strike dismay into the hearts of that confident
fraternity, but up to the present there has been no
sign of collapse. Still, Mr. Ahmad is no doubt a
learned Mohammedan who has popularised some
of the occultism of the school of thought to which
he belongs, and, its truth apart, it forms an interesting
narrative of the superstition attached essentially to
numbers.

But how did the notion arise? Probably from
the observation of coincidences, on which were
based the so-called laws of numbers. I will here
give some instances from quite recent history, for
which I am indebted to *Credulities Past and Present*.
The French nation of all classes are very much
given to the art of tracing prophetical references
in the numbers composing dates. French journals
have noticed the numerical prophecy of the termination
of the Empire in 1869. This small problem in
arithmetical divination was worked out thus :—
Napoleon III. was born in 1808, and assumed the

Empire in 1852. Add 1 + 8 + 0 + 8 to 1852 and 1869 results. Similarly, the Empress Eugenie was born in 1826, and married to the Emperor in 1853. The ciphers added together in each date give 1869, when added to 1852. The corresponding dates and events in the life of Louis Philippe, when dealt with in the same way, give the corresponding prophetical result.

The date of the great Revolution is 1789. Add to 1789 the sum of its ciphers and 1814 results— the date of the Fall of the Empire, which arose out of the Revolution. The date of the last Revolution is 1848, and if this date be similarly dealt with it gives as the prophetical result 1869. A writer in *Notes and Queries* (3rd Ser. vol. x.) remarks that these extraordinary numbers appear to have started with the accession to the throne of Louis XVI. in 1744 : by adding these figures into each other you get the date of his death, or $1774 + 1 + 7 + 7 + 4 = 1793$, in which year, January 21st, the amiable monarch was beheaded. Again, the Fall of Robespierre, 1794: add $1 + 7 + 9 + 4 = 1815$, gives that of Napoleon I. re-abdicating, June 22nd, 1815 ; add to this $1 + 8 + 1 + 5 = 1830$, which in its turn gives us the three glorious days of July and Fall of Charles X. Then we have accession of the Citizen King in 1830, thus :—

The date of his birth, October 6 $\left\{\begin{array}{r} 1830 \\ 1 \\ 7 \\ 7 \\ 3 \end{array}\right.$

$$\overline{1848}$$

Birth of his Queen, Marie Amélie, ⎰ 1830
April 26 ⎱ 1
7
8
2
_____
1848

Marriage of Louis Philippe, ⎰ 1830
November 25 ⎱ 1
8
0
9
_____
1848

Then came Universal Suffrage, December 10 and 11, and choice of a President of a Republic, one and indivisible, or

1848
1
8
4
8
_____
1869 Dec.

But the figures work out more remarkably thus :—
Louis Napoleon was proclaimed Emperor, January 30, 1853.

	1853			1853
	1			1
His birth,	8	Birth of Empress,		8
April 20	0	May 5		2
	8			6
	_____			_____
	1870			1870

Now, if a modern arithmetician can trace destiny in the figures of personal history with such an array of seeming, does it not follow that the older and more philosophical mathematician, noting the same coincidences in the events of his own day, was led to theorise on the fundamental nature of numbers ; his conclusions being that numbers are not mere no-things, but occult factors in life ; in a word, the bearers of fate or fortune ? He gave numbers to the planets, to letters, to words, to ideas ; and having plenty of time on his hands he elaborated the scheme until it became the occult thing as we know it to-day. Our modern belief in lucky numbers can have no other origin than that of coincidences we have noticed, or which we have accepted on the *ipse dixit* of some fortune-teller, following the rules of the Chaldeans or some other ancient people. As to the array of figures respecting Napoleon, it is sufficient to say that similar figures can be produced respecting lives on the ordinary plane of existence, just as readily as where there is no such show of mathematical logic. In fact, in nine cases out of ten the figures, like the answer of the schoolboy's problem, " won't work out." Almost as good a case in the literary world could be hatched up from a cipher in Hall Caine's works to prove they were written by Marie Corelli. For thousands of years the world has been taught that letters have numbers which exert a positive influence in life's affairs, deciding matters of high importance as well as the trivialities about which we do not care. But no evidence is offered by the authors of modern books as to the occult powers of numbers in themselves. O Hashnu Hara in *Number, Name and Colour* admits that the values of numbers of the Greek, Hebrew, and Arabic alphabets are different, so that it is pitch and toss as to which we are to take. Mr W. Wynne Westcott has written a more philosophical book on the subject, but even he has no satisfactory evidence to produce except this : that Pythagoras or somebody else "said" so. The revival of this superstition apparently means no more than its popularity as a social diversion.

(10) AMULETS, GEMS, CHARMS, TALISMANS, MASCOTS.

An amulet (from the Arab word hamala=to carry) is anything hung round the neck, placed like a bracelet on the wrist, or otherwise attached to the person, as an imagined preservative against sickness or other evils ; a charm is exactly the same thing, the only difference being that the word itself contains the notion of some human action imparting to the article a certain power for good—hence the expression, "a charmed life ;" a gem is simply the general name of a precious stone, used in this association because of alleged occult powers ; a talisman is a special kind of charm on which is cut or engraved a magical figure, worn to avoid disaster to the wearer. A mascot is identical with a talisman, except that the design need not be there. It will thus be seen that there is no essential difference between these articles : they are all worn to ward off diseases and bad luck.

Since the practice of wearing such protective devices is a very ancient one, and one that still obtains, with perhaps a tendency to increase, I propose to enquire into the habits of the past and of the present, and into the underlying reasons which are given by wearers for the use of charms and amulets. For it is not without significance that a West End lady should appear to have the same belief in their efficacy as a Priestess of Amen Ra, on whose remains are found evidences of careful protections against evil. A superstition that has vitality after the lapse of many thousands of years is worth more than ordinary attention.

Mr G. H. Bratley, the author of *The Power of Gems and Charms*, devotes no less than 94 pages to " Historical Charms," having collected together a great variety of cases to show the place which such objects have had in history. One must admit that certain articles have attained historic importance, mainly the articles which are said to exercise a malevolent influence, like the famous Spanish opal or the mummy case in the British Museum. What is lacking in the book under notice is *attestation*. For instance, no authority is given for the following story :—" The Czar of Russia is said to have great confidence in relics. He wears a ring in which is embedded a piece of the true Cross, and it is said to have the virtue of shielding its wearer from any physical danger. It was originally one of the treasures of the Vatican, and was presented to an ancestor of the Czar for diplomatic reasons. The value which its owner sets upon the ring is shewn by the fact that he will never, if possible, move any distance without it. Some years ago he was travelling from St Petersburg to Moscow, when he suddenly discovered he had forgotten the ring. The train was stopped immediately, and a special messenger sent

back in an express for it; nor would the Czar allow
the train to move until eight hours afterwards,
when the messenger returned with the ring.   It
is said that when his ill-fated grandfather was so
cruelly assassinated, he had left the ring behind him."
Very interesting as a story, but how do we know it is
true?   How do we know a good many other amulet
stories are true?   We *don't* know ; we only know there
is a considerable amount of literature to prove that
charms and amulets have been worn from time
immemorial.   That they are still worn, a little shyly,
a little half ashamedly, at least by Anglo-Saxons,
is quite true.   The man and woman from the West
End will wear their charms secretly as they listen
to the turns on the music-hall stage ; but the Asiatic
wrestler, who has discarded most of his clothing, still
wears his talisman round his neck—boldly, even
proudly.   He has a full-hearted belief in its efficacy
in spite of an occasional defeat ; the Anglo-Saxon is
not so sure, but with commercial instinct rather
than religious feeling, he wants to get the benefit
if there is one.   The psychological attitude is well
stated by a writer in *The Referee*, quoted by Mr
Bratley.   " The belief in mascottes or talismans is
very popular.   Charms, in the form of horse-shoes,
pigs, four-leaved clover, and countless other fancies,
are very general, and at present very fashionable.
I have worn a lucky bean for seven years, and never
lost it.   I should very much dislike to part with
it, and have a sort of half belief in its bringing
me luck, or at least keeping off ill-luck."   Exactly.
A " half-belief : no more than that.   The little pig
dangling from a lady's bracelet is there because

of a *hope* that it will bring good things. Ask her for
the underlying science and she will only smile.
" You do not understand." We are not dealing with
matters of common-sense, but with intuition. We
are following instinct rather than logic. Yes, we are,
when we wear trinkets and do not know why, except
that others have worn them thousands of years
ago and allege their potent influence for good. Is
not the secret of their power in the fact that they
are a visible emblem of defence? Take a Turkish
wrestler who wears his amulet round his neck. To
be without it would mean distress of mind—a real
state of fear; to have it is to bring out the best of his
powers. And yet his opponent, utterly destitute of
a charm or of a belief in them, will probably beat him
in the struggle. Belief in the charm will not
therefore be destroyed; the cause of the failure
will be looked for elsewhere.

The popularity of talismans, charms, amulets, and
the whole tribe of " lucky " gems, is best explained by
the fact that mankind is fond of decorative effect.
We may laugh at the naked savage, who will strut up
and down the deck of a trading steamer at Lorenzo
Marques, on which he is a visitor for a quarter of an
hour, dressed in a pair of spats and an old silk hat—
not a stitch of anything else—but there is the same
passion in more civilised countries. We express that
passion with more artistic restraint and better taste,
but with women especially the so-called belief in the
occult influence of charms is secondary to the love of
gold and silver trinkets by way of adornment. It
would not be true to say that the essential superstition is absent; there can be no doubt it would live

even though the trinket were ugly and objectionable. What we mean is that the decorative feature of charms comes first, because it addresses itself to the eye ; the appeal to fear and imagination comes later. Besides which, the curious details of how precious stones may be worn to evolve lucky events are worthy of an expert advertising agent who wanted to bring the best results for his clients—the goldsmiths and the jewellers. That some stones may be worn by everybody with advantage is a judicious statement, especially as those stones are diamonds, turquoises, and emeralds ;[1] but there is a difference of opinion as to what stones " govern " the month of the year. The usual scheme is as follows :—

Jan. = Garnet.	May = Emerald.	Sep. = Sapphire.
Feb. = Amethyst.	June = Agate.	Oct. = Opal.
Mar. = Bloodstone.	July = Ruby.	Nov. = Topaz.
April = Diamond.	Aug. = Sardonyx.	Dec. = Turquoise.

But Mr H. Stanley Redgrove, B.Sc., in an article in *The Occult Review* on " The Belief in Talismans," has a different arrangement, which, apparently, possesses antique authority at least equal to those one finds in such books as Brewer's *Dictionary of Phrase and Fable*, or an *Occult Encyclopædia*. Probably an acute astrologer would object to *all* the lists because they did not deal with "cusps." However, on the following page will be found an outline of Mr Redgrove's plan :—

Power of Gems and Charms, p. 128.

Sign of the Zodiac.	Astro-logical Symbol.	Month (commencing about the 21st of preceding month).	Stone.
Aries, the Ram - -	♈	April	Amethyst
Taurus, the Bull - -	♉	May	Agate
Gemini, the Twins -	♊	June	Beryl
Cancer, the Crab - -	♋	July	Emerald
Leo, the Lion - - -	♌	August	Ruby
Virgo, the Virgin - -	♍	September	Jasper
Libra, the Balance -	♎	October	Diamond
Scorpio, the Scorpion -	♏	November	Topaz
Sagittarius, the Archer	♐	December	Carbuncle
Capricorn, the Goat -	♑	January	Onyx
			Chalcedony
Aquarius, the Water-bearer - - - -	♒	February	Sapphire
Pisces, the Fishes - -	♓	March	Chrysolite

Mr Bratley appears to have made a compromise, for his list joins up half months in the following manner :—

Duration of Size and Sun's period therein.	Gem.
January 21 to February 18 - -	Garnet
February 19 to March 20 - - -	Amethyst
March 21 to April 20 - - - -	Bloodstone
April 21 to May 21 - - - - -	Sapphire
May 22 to June 21 - - - - -	Emerald
June 22 to July 23 - - - - -	Agate
July 24 to August 23 - - - -	Ruby

Duration of Size and Sun's period therein.	Gem.
August 24 to September 23 - -	Sardonyx
September 24 to October 23 - -	Chrysolite
October 24 to November 22 - -	Opal
November 23 to December 22 -	Topaz
December 23 to January 20 - -	Turquoise

Now, what is a woman to do who wishes to buy a ring with the right birth-stone in it? She was born on July 2nd, 1890. Has she to follow the first list? or the second? or the third? Who made these lists, and on what science are they founded? All Mr Bratley can say is they are formulated "according to the laws of judicial astrology." Is that all? If it is, then we may be sure a well educated girl, who has gone through some science and logic, will buy the ring for its beauty and intrinsic value first; the super-stitious element only provides her with material for Society small talk. Authors may fling quotations at us from Cornelius Agrippa, Paracelsus, and Madame Blavatsky, but we need better evidence than those people can furnish before we can accept the occult power of gems. Mr Stanley Redgrove is of opinion that the power is not in the charm, but in the belief of the wearer of the charm. It is the power of the *idea*, although there is some evidence which suggests the possibility of imparting certain mental qualities to an object.[1] This *idea* is all-sufficient, and an instance is quoted from an eminent anthropologist— Dr. Haddon, see his *Magic and Fetishism*—about a Congo negro, "who, being on a journey, lodged at a friend's house; the latter got a wild hen for his

[1] Pedsychometry, if studicarefully, provides material for this belief.

breakfast, and the young man asked if it were a wild hen? His host answered 'No.' Then he fell on heartily, and afterwards proceeded on his journey. After four years these two met together again, and his old friend asked him ' if he would eat a wild hen,' to which he answered that it was taboo to him. Hereat the host began immediately to laugh, inquiring of him, ' What made him refuse it now, when he had eaten one at his table four years ago ? ' At the hearing of this the negro immediately fell a-trembling, and suffered himself to be so far possessed with the effects of imagination that he died in less than twenty-four hours after."

Mr Redgrove thus concludes :—" We think, however, that the hidden truth underlying the mass of superstitious nonsense connected with the subject may be formulated thus :—*the power of the talisman is the power of the mind (or ' imagination') brought into activity by a suitable symbol.*

(11) OMENS—*Introductory.*

An omen is an event which is supposed to indicate destiny, the chief feature being the gratuitous nature of the happening ; it is a message about the future which we do not seek for. There is no origin for omens ; they are as old as man himself. From time immemorial the changing aspects of Nature have told him about the changes which may happen in his own life ; the flight of birds, the mysteries of dreams, a rabbit crossing the path, and an infinity of other matters have been taken as "signs" of something that forbodes good or ill—generally ill—a testimony to the almost universal fear with which man has regarded the forces surrounding his life.   Dryden and Lee in the *Œdipus* set forth the superstitions of their time :—

> "For when we think fate hovers o'er our heads,
>   Our apprehensions shoot beyond all bounds,
>   Owls, ravens, crickets seem the watch of death ;
>   Nature's worst vermin scare her godlike sons,
>   Echoes, the very leavings of a voice,
>   Grow babbling ghosts and call us to our graves :
>   Each mole-hill thought swells to a huge Olympus,
>   While we, fantastic dreamers, heave, and puff,
>   And sweat with an imagination's weight ;
>   As if, like Atlas, with these mortal shoulders
>   We could sustain the burden of the world."

It is useless to say that omens are going out of fashion ; they are still operative.   When the Liberals are turned out of office and at the election make a clean sweep of the first day's pollings, they do not hesitate to regard it as a good omen ; and the Conservatives are by no means backward in using the same phraseology if events for them should be equally propitious.   But it is in the mental and social life of the people that augury in the strict sense has its fullest scope, and in the sections that follow some proof of this statement will be forthcoming.

(12) LOOKING-GLASS OMENS.

To let a mirror fall and be broken is even now regarded as unfortunate, though not so ill-starred an accident as among the people of earlier days, who believed that the party to whom the mirror belonged would lose his best friend.

In the *Mémoires de Constant, premier Valet de Chambre de l'Empereur sur la Vie privée de Napoleon,* (Paris, 1830), Buonaparte's superstition respecting the looking-glass is particularly mentioned :—" During one of his campaigns in Italy he broke the glass over Josephine's portrait.   He never rested till the return of the courier he forthwith despatched to assure himself of her safety, so strong was the impression of her death upon his mind."

The origin of this superstition is very simple. Looking-glasses are and always have been implements of divination ; to break one is therefore accounted most disastrous, because it is the destruction of a means of knowing the will of the gods.   In his *Greek Antiquities*, Potter says :—" When divination by water was performed with a looking-glass, it was called *Catoptromancy* : sometimes they dipped a looking-glass into the water, when they desired to know what would become of a sick person : for as he looked well or ill in the glass, accordingly they presumed of his future condition.   Sometimes, also, glasses were used, and the images of what should happen, without water."   We need not go to Greek antiquity for divination by looking-glasses : a taxi-cab to several streets in the West End of London would bring us to the rooms of seers and seeresses, who will tell fortunes by Indian mirrors and the common or garden crystal gazing.

(13) STUMBLING AND FALLING.

When Julius Cæsar landed at Adrumetum in Africa, he tripped and fell on his face.   This would have been considered a fatal omen by his army, but with admirable presence of mind he exclaimed, " Thus I take possession of thee, O Africa."   When William the Conqueror leaped upon the shore at Bulverhythe, he fell on his face, and a great cry went forth that it was an ill omen; but the Duke exclaimed, " I have taken seisin of this land with both my hands."

Stumbling and falling, as omens, have what may be called a natural basis in thought, for, as in the cases just mentioned, there is a keen attention directed to the initial stages of any enterprise; even to-day the sudden shining of the sun on a hitherto cloudy day has been known to be taken as a good augury by people who are celebrating the foundation stone-laying of a new church; and although the visitation of a thunderstorm would not make them think the Deity was angry, they are quite ready to accept what seems like a happy circumstance. *Falling*, in other connections, has the significance that it has in the case of personal falls. This is seen in what may be called picture omens.

Archbishop Laud, not long before the disastrous circumstances happened which hastened his tragical end, on entering his study one day, found his picture at full length on the floor, the string which held it fastened to the wall having snapped. The sight of this struck the prelate with such an awing sense of the probability of his fate, that from that moment he never enjoyed a moment's peace. It, moreover, brought back to his mind a disaster that had occurred to one of his boats on the very day of his translation to the See of Canterbury, which sank with his coaches and horses into the Thames. The Duke of Buckingham was struck by an occurrence of a similar kind: he found his picture in the council chamber fallen out of its frame. This accident, in

M

that age of omens, was looked upon with a considerable degree of awe.

The logic of these situations seems to be that a fall of any kind is, if not a catastrophe in itself, the outward sign of one that is to come. When Laud found every picture hanging and intact except his own, it was natural that he should inquire why this should be so; and in days when the superstitious mind was *cultivated*, one can realise how serious reflections would arise and fears assert themselves. In some parts of England the sudden and unexplained falling of window blinds is regarded in the same prophetic light. As a superstition, it is to be accounted for on the same psychological basis, namely, that a fall, sudden and unexpected, strikes the mind by that very reason as the act of some unseen agency. In these enlightened days the falling window blind causes, for the most part, no more thought than a passing complaint on the workmanship of the house furnisher; but with ignorant and superstitious people, on the eternal look-out for signs, it will act as it did in the past: *something is going to happen.* When Mungo Park took his leave of Sir Walter Scott, prior to his second and fatal expedition to Africa, his horse stumbled on crossing a ditch which separated the moor from the road. "I am afraid," said Scott, "this is a bad omen." Park answered, smiling, "Omens follow them who look to them," and striking spur into his horse, galloped off. Scott never saw him again.

This is the kind of story which keeps the superstition pot a-boiling. The fearful reader says, "Ah!

he defied the omen, and Scott never saw him again."
But how many people have died tragically who
never stumbled, either on foot or when on horseback?

(14) SPILLING THE SALT.

If, whilst at dinner, you should be so unfortunate
as to spill the salt, and it falls *towards* your right-
hand or left-hand neighbour, it is accounted an
unlucky omen. Why, nobody can say—with any
show of good reasoning. Salt has always figured
prominently in religious rites and ceremonies. Both
Greeks and Romans mixed salt with their sacrificial
cakes, being, as an element, a necessary concomitant
of the sacrifice, not a mere adjunct. Thus in the
Ferialia, or offerings to the Diis Manibus, when no
animal was slain :

> "The Manes' rights expenses small supply,
> The richest sacrifice is piety.
> With vernal garlands a small Tile exalt,
> A little flour and little grain of Salt."

That the flour and salt were both designed as
propitiatory offerings to redeem them from the
vengeance of the Stygian or infernal gods, may
be proved from a like custom in the Lemuria,
another festival to the same Diis Manibus, where
beans are flung instead of the flour and salt ; and
when flung, the person says :

> "And with these beans I me and mine redeem."

That a Pagan should come to regard salt as an
emblem of redemptive power is, therefore, not surprising ; and from this it is but a step to the belief
that a spilling of it at table should be an omen of
serious import. In olden times salt was regarded as

incorruptible, and it became the symbol of friendship ; consequently an overturning of the salt-cellar betokened the breaking of friendship. But there was a "counter" stroke available. If the man towards whom the salt falls will, without hesitation or remark, take up a single pinch of salt between the finger and the thumb of his right hand and cast it over his left shoulder, the threatened misfortune will be averted. Tradition has it that the left shoulder is selected to appease the devil.[1]

Such superstitions are among those complex growths of ideas, the disentanglement of which is quite an impossibility. There are nations to whom salt was an almost sacred symbol ; there are others— Egypt, for instance—to whom it was a common metaphor for calamity and desolation. But as a superstition it has some peculiar, insistent force, for the spilling of salt is a common accident, and it is by no means uncommon to see the rite of throwing over the left shoulder carried out immediately ; not, it is true, with any real fear of evil, but in order, as one lady put it, "to be on the safe side." Some writers believe that da Vinci's picture of the Last Supper, in which Judas Iscariot is represented as overturning the salt, is the real origin of the salt superstition.

(15) THIRTEEN AT TABLE.

If you care to take the trouble, you can work up a really awe-inspiring amount of evidence to show that it is unlucky to sit thirteen at table ; and when the daring of Matthew Arnold in defying the superstition

[1] Owen, *On Serpents.*

is told in all its solemnity—he died within a year
after the event—even solid people shudder and begin
to think "there is something in it." Quite sensible
women shrink in horror from a thirteen table, and
imagine the addition of a fourteenth person will
break the evil spell, rendering it inoperative. Of
course the origin of the superstition is the Last
Supper, where thirteen were present; and the
tragedies subsequent to that meal are supposed to be
repeated every time its number is enacted. What a
frightful slaughter would have marked the course of
civilisation had this been true! But Quetelet, in his
Theory of Probabilities has, one would have thought,
smashed the idea beyond hope of revival. He says :
—"There is a prejudice existing generally on the
pretended danger of being *the thirteenth at table.* If
the probability be required that out of thirteen
persons of different ages, one of them, at least, shall
die within a year, it will be found that the chances
are about one to one that one death at least will
occur. This calculation by means of a false interpretation has given rise to the prejudice, no less
ridiculous, that the danger will be avoided by inviting
a greater number of guests which can only have the
effect of augmenting the probability of the event so
much apprehended." This is sound logic ; so very
different from the blind reasoning of fanciful people
who think that in some occult manner a tragedy of
the past will be repeated, if the same number of people
congregate together for the evening meal. The
superstition of thirteen at table is one of the most
pitiful exhibitions of mental weakness that has ever
marked human thought. "Thirteen Clubs," com-

posed of men and women determined to defy the
superstition, may justify themselves as social diver-
sions, but as serious attempts at what is called dis-
proof, they are as futile as might be expected. Below
I give an extract from a London newspaper :—

" NEW YORK, Jan. 16.
"Superstition was flouted and invited to do its
worst by all manner of taunts levelled against the
fearsome number thirteen at a banquet given in New
York last night by the members of the Thirteen Club.

" The club contains many more than thirteen
members, but the diners sat at tables thirteen to each.
Before each plate a red candle burned in a death's
head holder, and the member whose candle went out
first was supposed to receive it as a sign. As soon as
the company was seated a new mirror was broken.

" The ices were served in the form of a skull
reposing in a coffin. The toastmaster used a forearm
bone to rap for order. At intervals the diners counted
up to thirteen as a chant, the number thirteen being
hailed with cheers.

" At the close of the banquet the waiters filed into
the room to the music of a funeral march, each
waiter bearing aloft a chocolate cake with thirteen
candles burning on it and a white skull and cross-
bones in the centre.

" Insulted fate had revenge on the diners at one of
the tables. At the head of each table an open
umbrella was placed to flaunt the rain superstition.
A waiter bearing a well-filled soup tureen caught the
tail of his coat in one of the umbrellas, and there was
a shower of hot soup over some of the jesters."

Yes, superstition *was* flouted, and so was intelligence.

(16) THE OWL.

Bourne remarks that " if an owl, which is reckoned a most abominable and unlucky bird, send forth its hoarse and dismal voice, it is an omen of the approach of some terrible thing ; that some dire calamity and some great misfortune is near at hand." This omen occurs in Chaucer :

> " The jelous Swan, ayenst hys deth that singeth,
> The *Oule* eke, that of deth the bode bringeth."
>
> *Assembly of Foules.*

It is thus mentioned by Spenser :

> " This rueful Strich still wayting on the beere,
> The whistler shril, that whoso heares doth die."

It would be too much to say that these sentiments are still alive to-day, but it is not too much to say that women and children listen to the weird cries with something approaching apprehension. Why ? Simply because the note is dismal, and because it is heard in the night when other sounds are still. And if such is the effect now, we need not be surprised to learn it was the effect in more superstitious ages ; ages when men, too, were under the spell. An owl once strayed into the Capitol at Rome, with the result that the city underwent a lustration. Butler speaks of this incident in his *Hudibras* :—

> " The Roman Senate, when within
> The city walls an Owl was seen,
> Did cause their clergy with lustrations
> (Our Synod calls humiliations)
> The round-fac'd prodigy t'avert
> From doing town and country hurt."

The Romans appear to have had most determined views on owls and their significance. "Julius Obsequens (in his *Book of Prodigies*, c. 85) shews that a little before the death of Commodus Antoninus, the Emperor, an Owl was observed to sit upon the top of his chamber, both at Rome and at Lanuvium. Xiphilinus, speaking of the prodigies that went before the death of Augustus, says that the Owl sang upon the top of the Curia. He shews, also, that the Actian War was presignified by the flying of Owls into the Temple of Concord. In the year 1542, at Herbipolis, or Wirtz-burg, in Franconia, this unlucky bird, by his screeching songs, affrighted the citizens a long time together, and immediately followed a great plague, war, and other calamities. About twenty years ago, I did observe that in the house where I lodged, an Owl, groaning in the window, presaged the death of two eminent persons, who died there shortly after."

The death of such convictions could not fail to be slow, but widening knowledge has at last almost dispersed them, and nothing is left but the weird screech itself.

(17) THE HOWLING OF DOGS.

The author of *Arcana Microcosmi* (1652) affirms with a curiously quaint confidence that "dogs by their howling portend death and calamities is plaine by historie and experience." Shakespeare in his *Henry* VI. dares to use the custom as an accompaniment of birth.

> "The owl shriek'd at thy birth, an evil sign!
> The night-crow cry'd aboding luckless time,
> *Dogs howl'd*, and hideous tempests shook down trees."

The *British Apollo* (1708) answering the question " Whether the dogs howling may be a fatal prognostic, or no," says : " We cannot determine, but 'tis probable that out of a sense of sorrow for the sickness or absence of his master, or the like, that creature may be so disturbed." Another writer concludes :—" I have some little faith in the howling of a dog, when it does not proceed from hunger, blows, or confinement. As odd and unaccountable as it may seem, those animals scent death, even before it seizes a person."

This is superstition *in excelsis.* Animals—horses for instance—have been seen to tremble when they came near a dead human body, even though the body was invisible to them ; but scenting death is quite a different thing. And yet there is reason to believe that this alleged power is the basis of the popular belief in the howling of dogs. Even in the *Odyssey* the dogs of Eumæus are described as terrified at the sight of Minerva, though she was then invisible to Telemachus. If so far back in the ages the canine tribe were endowed, in human thought at least, with such vision, it can be understood how their supposed distressful howling should presage death, especially in houses where somebody is lying ill. But the real truth probably lies in this : that there are influences in the atmosphere which act upon dogs in a way which causes them to howl, but which we do not understand. Willsford, in his *Nature's Secrets*, says that when " dogs tremble and wallow upon the earth . . are signs of rain and wind for certain." This may be as much a superstition as the other, but there is no doubt that cattle have a physical sensitiveness to

coming storms which men are destitute of, and
drovers in the Far West watch their stock during
dangerous weather seasons for this very reason. That
somebody should die after the continued howling of
a dog is not a remarkable phenomenon ; the remarkable phenomenon is the number of people who live
after listening to many howlings.

(18) Ear-Tingling.

In Shakespeare's *Much Ado about Nothing*, Beatrice
says :—" What fire is in mine ears ! " which Warburton
explains as alluding to a proverbial saying of the
common people, that their ears burn when others
are talking of them. On which Reed observes
that the opinion from whence this proverbial saying
is derived is of great antiquity, being thus mentioned
by Pliny :—" Moreover is not this an opinion generally
received, that when our ears do glow and tingle some
there be that in our absence doe talk of us ? " Sir
Thomas Browne says :—" When our cheek burns, or
ear tingles, we usually say somebody is talking of us,
a conceit of great antiquity, and ranked among
superstitious opinions by Pliny. He supposes it to
have proceeded from the notion of a signifying genius,
or universal mercury that conducted sounds to their
distant subjects and taught to hear by touch." " My
ears tingle ; somebody is talking against me," is a
remark one can hear even to-day ; and although, as
in many other cases, it is made to be laughed at, there
is a kind of private fancy that the superstition " may
have something in it." That something is an illusion
of analogy ; for if you give a man a sharp rebuke for
carelessness, you make his ears tingle, as a rule ; and

when his ears tingle and you are not present in the
body, he presumes you *are* present in mind. Thus
Herrick in his *Hesperides* :

ON HIMSELFE.
"One Eare tingles, some there be
That are snarling now at me;
Be they those that Homer bit,
I will give them thanks for it."

(19) SNEEZING.

The advance of modern physiology has all but
killed the sneezing superstition, at least in civilised
countries. Among peoples who have not emerged
from savagery, or whose intellectual equipment, in
spite of contact with superior races, is still meagre in
the extreme, sneezing is an omen whose significance
they dare not disallow. It might not be too much to
say that there are white races who look upon the
sneeze of a sick child as an omen. Even the Christian
world at one time was a devout supporter of the
sneezing superstition. Probably there are people
living to-day who can remember the "God bless
you," which was usually addressed to a person after a
sneeze. The origin of the saying is found by some
authorities in the fact that "violent sneezing was once
an epidemic and mortal distemper from whence the
custom took its rise. In one of Martial's epigrams
we find the Romans had the same custom, and not
improbably derived from the same reason." But the
real origin lies in the doctrine of the soul as understood by primitive man. Some approach to this
fact is attained in the translation by Sir Henry Ellis
of a section from Garnier's *History of France* :—

" The year 750 is commonly reckoned the era of

the custom of saying 'God bless you' to one who happens to sneeze. It is said that, in the time of the pontificate of St Gregory the Great, the air was filled with such a deleterious influence that they who sneezed immediately expired. On this the devout pontiff appointed a form of prayer, and a wish to be said to persons sneezing for averting them from the fatal effects of this malignancy. A fable contrived against all the rules of probability, it being certain that this custom has from time immemorial subsisted in all parts of the known world. According to mythology, the first sign of life Prometheus's artificial man gave was by sternutation. This supposed creator is said to have stolen a portion of the solar rays ; and filling with them a phial, which he had made on purpose, sealed it up hermetically. He instantly flies back to his favourite automaton, and opening the phial, held it close to the statue ; the rays, still retaining all their activity, insinuate themselves through the pores, and set the fictitious man a-sneezing. Prometheus, transported with the success of his machine, offers up a fervent prayer with wishes for the preservation of so singular a being. His automaton observed him, remembering his ejaculations, was very careful on the like occasions to offer these wishes in behalf of his descendants, who perpetuated it from father to son in all their colonies.

"The Rabbies, speaking of this custom, do likewise give it a very ancient date. They say that, not long after the Creation, God made a general decree that every man living should sneeze but once, and that at the very instant of his sneezing his soul should depart without any previous indisposition. Jacob by no means liked so precipitate a way of leaving the world, as being desirous of settling his family affairs and those of his conscience : he prostrated himself before the Lord, wrestled a second time with him, and earnestly entreated the favour of being excepted from the decree. His prayer was heard, and he sneezed without dying. All the Princes of the universe, being acquainted with the fact, unanimously ordered that, for the future, sneezing should be accompanied with thanksgivings for the preservation, and wishes for the prolongation, of life. We perceive, even in these fictions, the vestiges of tradition and history, which place the epocha of this civility long before that of Christianity. It was accounted very ancient even in the time of Aristotle, who, in his 'Problems,' has endeavoured to account for it, but knew nothing of its origin. According to him, the first men, prepossessed with the highest ideas concerning the head, as the principal seat of the soul, that intelligent substance governing and animating the whole human system, carried their respect even to sternutation, as the most manifest and most sensible operation of the head. Hence those several forms of compliments used on similar occasions amongst Greeks and Romans : *Long may you live! May you enjoy health! Jupiter preserve you!*"

But the true story of the sneezing superstition is told by Professor E. B. Tylor, who says :—

"In Asia and Europe the sneezing superstition extends through a wide range of race, age, and country. Among the passages relating to it in the classic ages of Greece and Rome, the following are some of the most characteristic : the lucky

sneeze of Telemachus in the Odyssey; the soldier's
sneeze and the shout of adoration to the god which
rose along the ranks, and which Xenophon appealed
to us a favourable omen; Aristotle's remark that
people consider a sneeze as divine, but not a cough;
the Greek epigram on the man with the long nose
who did not say Zeu Soson when he sneezed, for the
noise was too far off for him to hear; Petronius
Arbiter's mention of the custom of saying 'Salve'
to one who sneezed; and Pliny's question ' Cur
sternutamentis salutamus?' à-propos of which he
remarks that even Tiberius Caesar, that saddest
of men, exacted this observance. Similar rites
of sneezing have long been observed in Eastern
Asia. When a Hindu sneezes, bystanders say
'Live!' and the sneezer replies, 'With you!' It is
an ill omen to which among other things the Thugs
paid great regard on starting an expedition, and
which even compelled them to let the travellers
with them escape[1]." But this does not show us
the real origin of the sneezing superstition; although
it adequately shews the extent of its operations.
Tylor traces the first beginnings of the habit in
the savage idea of souls. "As a man's soul is
considered to go in and out of his body, so it is with
other spirits, particularly such as enter into patients
and possess them or afflict them with disease. Among
the less cultured races the connection of this idea with
sneezing is best shewn among the Zulus, a people
firmly persuaded that kindly or angry spirits of the
dead hover about them in dreams, enter into them
and cause disease in them. When a Zulu sneezes he

[1] Tylor, *Primitive Culture*, vol. i. p. 100.

will say, 'I am now blessed. The Idhlozi (ancestral spirit) is with me ; it has come to me. Let me hasten and praise it, for it is it which causes me to sneeze.' So he praises the manes of his family, asking for cattle, and wives and blessings."

Thus from the far past, as seen in the customs of uncivilised races in the present, must we draw the solution of a curious superstition, one which, better perhaps than any other that could be mentioned, is a good illustration of the power of ignorance to create and foster a delusion. Even the great Aristotle indulged in the problem as to "why sneezing from noon to midnight was good, but from night to noon unlucky." If "the master of those who know" could be puzzled by a physiological simplicity, shall we be amazed at the extent of the sneezing superstition throughout the long centuries of pagan and Christian history?

(20) SPITTING.

The present writer can remember labourers in the North of England who were in the habit of spitting on a coin "for luck," especially if it were a coin they found on the highway. To trace this habit to its source is practically impossible. Spittle among the ancients was esteemed a Charm against all kinds of fascination : so Theocritus,

> "Thrice on my breast I spit to guard me safe
> From fascinating Charms."

And thus Persius upon the custom of Nurses spitting upon Children :

"See how old beldams expiations make:
To atone the Gods the Bantling up they take;
His lips are wet with lustral spittle, thus
They think to make the Gods propitious."

"Spitting, according to Pliny, was superstitiously observed in averting witchcraft and in giving a shrewder blow to an enemy. Hence seems to be derived the custom our Bruisers have of spitting in their hands before they begin their barbarous diversion, unless it was originally done for luck's sake. Several other vestiges of this superstition, relative to fasting Spittle, mentioned also by Pliny, may yet be placed among our vulgar customs.

The boys in the North of England have a custom amongst themselves of spitting their faith (or, as they call it in the northern dialect, "their Saul," *i.e.* Soul), when required to make asseverations in matters which they think of consequence.

In combinations of the colliers etc., about Newcastle-upon-Tyne, for the purpose of raising their wages, they are said to spit upon a stone together, by way of cementing their confederacy. Hence the popular saying, when persons are of the same party, or agree in sentiments, that 'they spit upon the same stone.'"

Probably this use of spittle is one of the few remainders left to us from a whole body of scatological rites, now happily dispensed with. A writer in *Notes and Queries* in 1868 says :—" I was, a few years ago, a clergyman of a parish within ten miles of Birmingham, much frequented on holidays by a low class of mechanics ; and I invariably noticed that, whenever I passed, some one or more of them spit aside ; giving one the idea that they

belonged to some sect, or society, which enjoined
the rule to spit whenever a clergyman passed, or
perhaps any known churchman."
This must have been coincidence, for there is
no trace of such a custom as spitting on passing
a parson. The superstition was rather in the cleric
than in the mechanics.

(21) KNIFE SUPERSTITIONS.

When little Teddy is being trained in table
manners, he is told it is improper to place his knife
and fork crosswise after the meal is finished; he
must place them side by side. Few people seem
to think there is anything behind this item of
etiquette; they imagine it is socially right because
the crosswise position is æsthetically wrong; it *looks*
ugly.

Again, if a friend makes you a present of a knife,
he invariably asks you for a halfpenny, because it
is accounted unlucky to *give* a knife to a friend; it
is apt to symbolise the cutting asunder of the bond
of union. Gay says :—

> " But woe is me ! such presents lucklesss prove,
> For knives, they tell me, always sever love."

The ritual of a past age was not wholly religious ;
it was to some extent secular, and the symbols of
things purely human. Hence to cross your knife
and fork at table is, according to Melton's *Astrolo-
gaster*, to invite crosses and misfortune, from which
we may presume that the mere mechanical position
of the cutlery was either suggestive of Calvary, or
symbolised troubles and crosses to come. How fer-

N

vently did our forefathers seek for types of the divine in the human, and of the moral in the material!

(22) Sharks Following Ships a Sign of Death.

It is an old but still operative superstition among seafaring men, or, shall I say, certain portions of them, that when a shark (or sharks) persistently follows a vessel, it is a sign that someone on board is going to die. The alleged reason is that the shark can "scent" death. The biography of the Rev. Bryan Roe, a West African missionary, contains the following narrative, which, when rid of the humorous exaggerations of the sailor, may be said to contain his point of view :—" Two or three sharks, it may be, are following in the vessel's wake, attracted, it would seem, by the fact that there is a sick man lying on board ; for the old, weather-beaten, quarter-master confidentially informs the clerical passenger (Mr Roe) that he will soon have a burial job on hand. The quarter-master is always an authority on the subject of sharks. ' Them there sharks,' he explains, ' have more sense in them than most Christchuns. They knows wot's wot, I can tell yer ; doctors ain't in it with sharks. I've heard sharks larf when the doctor has told a sick man he was convalescent— larf, sir, outright, 'cos they knew what a blessed mistake he was making. They are following up the scent of a man on board now that's going to die, and they'll not leave us until such times be as they get him.' "

Procter's *Return of the Admiral* is a good setting of the shark superstition :—

> " How gallantly, how merrily
> We ride along the sea.
> The morning is all sunshine,
> The wind is blowing free,
> The billows are all sparkling
> And bounding in the light.'

But

> " In our wake like any servant
> Follows ever the bold shark.

Then the admiral of the fleet who

> " Grew paler,
> And paler, as we flew,
> Spied the creature
> That kept following in our lee.

He seemed to be aware of the direful augury, for

> " *He shook*—'twas but an instant
> For speedily the pride
> Ran crimson to his heart,
> Till all chances he defied."

But the admiral's defiance was in vain, for

> " That night a hurried whisper
> Fell on us where we lay,
> And we knew our fine old admiral
> Was changing into clay.
> And we heard the wash of waters,
> Though nothing could we see,
> And a whistle and a plunge
> Among the *billows* in our lea;
> Till dawn we watched the body
> In its dead and ghastly sleep;
> And next evening, at sunset,
> It was slung into the deep.
> And never from that moment,
> Save *one* shudder through the sea,
> Saw we or heard the shark
> That had followed in our lee."

Mr Frank Gibson, to whose very interesting *Superstitions about Animals* I am indebted for the details of this subject, says that the superstition, so far as he knows, has no foundation in fact. Sharks follow in the wake of vessels for the same reason that all fish do, solely for the scraps of meat and other leavings that are thrown overboard. " On a voyage to South Africa, I noticed," remarks Mr Gibson, "when nearing the Equator, that a very large, sinister looking shark kept up with the vessel for many miles, but the passage concluded under the most favourable and happy circumstances ; no one died, and very few were even sea-sick. Curiously enough, however, when I returned to England on a large liner, fitted up as a hospital ship with accommodation for more than a thousand invalids, we never sighted a shark from Capetown to Southampton, though there were many cases of sickness on board, and *one of the passengers was buried at sea.*"

Truly this *ought* to have been a favoured vessel, but it seems to have escaped sharkly attentions. An isolated instance, however, will not extinguish the belief of a superstitious sailor, and we have still to answer the question as to how the idea arose. Probably it belongs to that group of beliefs which rest on the alleged powers of all kinds of animals, crediting them with a prescience in some respects superhuman. Thus the vulture is said, with some show of evidence, to know when death is likely to overtake the desert traveller ; the cattle on the prairie "scent" the storm long before the cowboy knows it is coming ; the howling dog presages death, and the attendant shark is credited with knowing more than the M.D. In the days of sailing vessels and slow voyages, the mariner was more superstitious than he is to-day, because he was more at the mercy of wind and weather ; and he had funerals at sea

often enough to support, if not originate, the superstition of the shark. The modern liner, with more
people aboard and more chances of death, harbours
no belief in the supernatural knowledge of fish, great
or small ; so many vessels are passing too and fro
that the shark has his pick of them, and need
not follow one for days together. But in past
centuries he had no such luck ; when he found a
sailing ship he stuck to it in the hope of finding
a meal, not of human flesh, but of anything he could
get hold of. And so many sharks followed so many
vessels in the course of years, that there was ample
room for the evolution of a superstition to the effect
that a persistent shark could scent death on board.

(23) BLACK CATS.

Black cats for luck : that is an old and an equally
modern superstition. But it must be really black,
with no admixture of other colours ; not even a
single hair. A lady who recently lost her cat said,
" I should not have minded, but it was *perfectly black*."
The following instance of a belief in black-cat luck
is taken from the *Badminton Magazine* (March,
1903) :—" The Prince (Ranjitsinghi) has a great
superstition in black cats, and the appearance of
one at a shooting gathering serves to convince him
in advance of a fine morning, plus a fine bag, and
singularly enough it always turns out so. Twice in
succession, he claims, has the timely appearance of
a black cat been instrumental in winning a county
match for Sussex, in addition to other occasions."
A superstitious belief in cats, black and otherwise, is
of great antiquity. Among the Egyptians the animals

were regarded with the utmost reverence, and their
mummified remains, a cargo of which was imported
to England not many years ago, are frequently found
in the same tombs as their worshippers. In witchcraft and soothsaying, cats have always played no
unimportant part, and wherever we see a picture or
description of a witch's hovel, there, too, we shall
certainly find portrayed her companion in darkness—
a black cat.

> " In a dirtie haire-lace
> She leads on a brace
> Of black-bore-cats to attend her ;
> Who scratch at the moone,
> And threaten at noone
> Of night from Heaven to render her."
> —HERRICK (" The Hag ").

One of the special ingredients in the filthy con-
coctions with which these hags were supposed to
work their villainy was the brains of a black cat.
Ben Jonson in his *Masque of Queens* mentions this
ingredient in the song sung by the witches :—

> " I from the jaws of a gardener's bitch,
> Did snatch these bones and then leaped the ditch ;
> Yet I went back to the house again,
> Killed the black cat, and here's the brain." [1]

The black cat has been accounted lucky from time
immemorial, but that is about all that can be traced.
There is no reason why this position should have
been assigned to him ; and of course the superstition
itself is an absurdity among the most illiterate of
its kind.

[1] For details in this section I am indebted to *Superstitions about
Animals.*

(24) THE CUCKOO.

The cuckoo has been long considered as a bird of omen. Gay, in his *Shepherd's Week*, in the fourth Pastoral, notes the vulgar superstitions on first hearing the bird sing in the season :—

> "When first the year, I heard the cuckoo sing,
> And call with welcome note the budding Spring,
> I straightway set a running with such haste,
> Deb'rah that won the smock scarce ran so fast.
> Till spent for lack of breath, quite weary grown,
> Upon a rising bank I sat adown,
> And doff'd my shoe, and by my troth I swear,
> Therein I spied this yellow frizzled hair,[1]
> As like to Lubberkin's in curl and hue,
> As if upon his comely pate it grew."

The present writer can remember that, during his youth in the North of England, boys on first hearing the cuckoo would take out of their pockets the money lying therein (if any) and spit on it for luck. The habit was not elegant, but Sir Henry Ellis refers to the practice as marking the northern counties in particular : "It is vulgarly accounted an unlucky omen if you have no money in your pocket when you hear the cuckoo for the first time in a season."

What is the origin of this superstition? It can only be this : that all birds signifying the advent of spring are regarded as welcome messengers of the return of life to the earth. They bring good news ; their coming is omen-ous of better things—like the coming of the swallow, who shares the good luck omen of the cuckoo.

[1] Thus described in *The Connoisseur*, No. 56 : "I got up last May Morning and went into the fields to hear the cuckoo, and when I pulled off my shoe I found a hair in it exactly the same colour with his."

(25) COMETS.

If the usual appearance of Nature was sufficiently
marvellous to beget all kinds of superstitions in the
mind of the untutored savage, it is only natural
that the sudden advent of a blazing comet in the
sky should affright him, and give rise to all kinds
of crude notions about coming disasters. To some
extent this is true of the civilised world, especially
that part of it which is morbidly religious and
dominated by prophecies respecting the Second
Coming of Christ. Take the year 1712. Whiston—
the mathematical divine, the translator of Josephus—
had predicted that the comet of 1712 would appear
on Wednesday, the 14th October, at five minutes
after five o'clock A.M.; and that the world would be
destroyed by fire on the Friday following. His
reputation for science was as high as his character
for orthodoxy was questionable, and the comet
appeared punctually—leading to an inferential fear
that the rest of the prediction would be as punctually
fulfilled. A number of persons got into boats and
barges in the Thames, thinking the water the safest
place. South Sea and India stock fell. The captain
of a Dutch ship threw all his powder into the river,
that the ship might not be endangered. At noon,
after the comet appeared, it is said that more than
one hundred clergymen were ferried over to Lambeth
Palace, to request that proper prayers might be
prepared, there being none in the church service
appropriate to such an emergency. People believed
that the Day of Judgment was at hand, and acted,
some on this belief, but more as if some temporary

evil was to be expected. Many wrongs were righted, many breaches of morality repaired. There was a great run on the bank; and Sir Gilbert Heathcote, at that time head director, issued orders to all the fire-offices in London, requesting them to keep a good look-out, and have a particular eye on the Bank of England. On the whole, the poor Londoners of that generation appear to have behaved rather foolishly in the moment of imagined doom.[1]

But in this year of grace 1910, when the daily press is full of references to the Miners' Comet and to Halley's Comet, there are semi-superstitious journalists and rabid politicians who are trying to see "signs" in the heavens. It is not a question of providing "copy" during the stress of a General Election, or of supplying notes about what happened when Halley's Comet appeared on previous occasions; the references were so put that the reader could not help getting the impression of a keen desire on the part of the writer to turn the comet into an omen of ill. We laugh at Whiston, but candidly we are not much better when we attempt to make political capital out of a star with a tail. Why not believe in astrology at once?

[1] From *Omens and Superstitions.*

MISCELLANEOUS

MISCELLANEOUS

(1) HOLY WELLS.

The Britisher acquainted with his Bible has an easy explanation of the superstitious regard for wells and fountains: "in hot and dry countries water is so valuable and necessary that the sources of the supply come to be looked upon as almost divine; verily the gifts of the gods. Whatever remnants of this superstition still remain are due to this natural cause." But such an explanation is quite inadequate, inasmuch as it merely accounts for the Eastern sense of water's value as an economic necessity. Over and above that, however, there is evidence to show that all nations have held wells and fountains in a kind of religious awe; in fact, the religious element has been uppermost, and although there is always an organic connection between the material benefit and the spiritual ideal, that connection is very slight in humid countries like Ireland, where at one time the worship of wells was as extravagant as anywhere in the Far East. On an island near the centre of Lough Fine there used to be a place for pilgrims anxious to get rid of their sins, the journey over the water being an important part of the business. It was believed to be easier to get rid of sin on an island than on the mainland. In Scotland (Tullie Beltane) there is a Druid temple of eight upright stones. Some distance away is another temple, and near it a well still held in great veneration, says a writer in *The Gentleman's Magazine* (1811). "On Beltane morning superstitious people go to this well and drink of it ; then they make a procession round it nine times ; after this they in like manner go round the temple. So deep-rooted is this heathenish superstition in the minds of many who reckon themselves good Protestants, that they will not neglect these rites even when Beltane falls on a Sabbath." Side by side with this account may be placed another (taken from *The Statistical Account of Scotland*, vol. XII., 1794). The place referred to is Kirkmichael, in Banff. "Near the kirk of this parish there is a fountain, once highly celebrated, and anciently dedicated to St Michael. Many a patient have its waters restored to health, and many more have attested the efficacy of their virtues. But, as the presiding power is sometimes capricious, and apt to desert his charge, it now lies neglected, choked with weeds, unhonoured and unfrequented. In better days, it was not so ; for the winged guardian, under the semblance of a fly, was never absent from his duty. If the sober matron wished to know the issue of her husband's ailment, or the love-sick nymph that of her languishing swain, they visited the well of St Michael. Every movement of the sympathetic fly was regarded in silent awe ; and as he appeared cheerful or dejected, the anxious votaries drew their presages ; their breasts vibrated with correspondent emotions. Like the Delai Lama of Thibet, or the King of Great Britain, whom a fiction of the English law supposes never to die, the guardian fly of the well of St Michael was believed to be exempted from the laws of mortality. To the eye of ignorance he might sometimes appear dead, but, agreeably to the Druidic system, it was only a transmigration into a similar form, which made little alteration on the real identity." " Not later than a fortnight ago" (it is added) " the writer of this account was much entertained to hear an old man lamenting with regret the degeneracy of the times, particularly the contempt in which objects of former veneration were held by the unthinking crowd. If the infirmities of years and the distance of his residence did not prevent him, he would still pay his devotional visits to the well of St Michael. He would clear the bed of its ooze, open a passage for the streamlet, plant the borders with fragrant flowers, and once more, as in the days of youth, enjoy the pleasure of seeing the guardian fly skim in sportive circles over the bubbling wave, and with its little proboscis imbibe the panacean dews."

In Wales, the same regard for Holy Wells is perhaps more distinctive than in other parts of the country, probably because the medical or curative properties have been more closely allied with the religious element. Holywell (or St. Winefred's) was a famous well for stricken pilgrims so far back as the fourteenth century, and the modern holiday-maker doing a North Wales tour, can still see the pilgrims of the day journeying to St. Winefred's, in the hope of leaving their troubles behind them. Pennant, in his

Tour in Wales, speaking of the village of Llandegla, where is a church dedicated to St. Tecla, virgin and martyr, who, after her conversion by St. Paul, suffered under Nero at Iconium, says :—" About two hundred yards from the church, in a quillet called Gwern Degla, rises a small spring. The water is under the tutelage of the saint, and to this day held to be extremely beneficial in the falling sickness. The patient washes his limbs in the well ; makes an offering into it of fourpence ; walks round it three times ; and thrice repeats the Lord's Prayer. These ceremonies are never begun till after sunset, in order to inspire the votaries with greater awe. If the afflicted be of the male sex, like Socrates, he makes an offering of a cock to his Æsculapius, or rather to Tecla, Hygeia ; if of the fair sex, a hen. The fowl is carried in a basket, first round the well, after that into the churchyard, when the same orisons and the same circum-ambulations are performed round the church. The votary then enters the church, gets under the communion-table, lies down with the Bible under his or her head, is covered with the carpet or cloth, and rests there till break of day, departing after offering sixpence, and leaving the fowl in the church. If the bird dies, the cure is supposed to have been effected, and the disease transferred to the devoted victim."

It would be possible to duplicate instances of this kind all over the country, but the most interesting cases are those relating to the superstition of decorating wells and fountains. Here is an illuminating letter from a correspondent of *The Gentleman's Magazine* (1794) :—

"Your correspondent F. J. having given you a short account of the custom still prevalent at Tissington, in Derbyshire, of decorating wells on Holy Thursday, please to inform him that it was anciently no uncommon practice; and two places in the county of Stafford instantly occurred to my recollection (Brewood and Bilbrook), where the same custom was observed of late years, if not at the present time. And I believe the same kind of ornaments were used to decorate all Gospel-places, whether wells, trees, or hills. In Popish times this respect was paid to such wells as were eminent for curing distempers upon the Saint's Day whose name the well bore, the people diverting themselves with cakes and ale, music and dancing; which was innocent enongh in comparison with what had been formerly practised at different places, when even the better sort of people placed a sanctity in them, brought alms and offerings, and made vows at them; as the ancient Germans and Britons did, and the Saxons and English were too much inclined to; for which St. Edmund's Well, near Oxford, and St. Lawrence's at Peterborough were once famous. This superstitious devotion, which was called well worship, was not approved of by the heads of the Church, and was strictly prohibited by our Anglican Councils: (1) under King Edgar; (2) under King Canute; (3) in a Council at London under St. Anselm, Archbishop of Canterbury, 1102; as it was also particularly at those two wells near Oxford and at Peterborough by Oliver Sutton, Bishop of Lincoln."

I propose now to give an account of how the Tissington Well was decorated, and then to enquire

O

into the origin of the ceremony itself. " The flowers were inserted in moist clay and put upon boards, cut in various forms, surrounded with boughs of laurel and white thorn, so as to give an appearance of water issuing from small grottoes. The flowers were adjusted and arranged in various patterns to give the effect of mosaic work, having inscribed upon them texts of Scripture appropriate to the season, and sentences expressive of the kindness of the Deity." The sams writer (1823) adds : " I will now proceed to give an account of the circumstances attendant on this annual festival on May 8, 1823, while I was on a visit at Ashburn with my friend, the Rev. Thomas Gibbs, second master of the Grammar School there, and curate of Tissington. There are five wells, and the Psalms appointed for the morning service, with the Epistle and Gospel for the day, being omitted at church, were read by Mr Gibbs, one at each well, when a Psalm was also sung by the parish choir. I officiated in the church, and preached a sermon on the occasion . . . from the church, the congregation walked to the first, or the Hall Well. As there is a recess at the back of the well, and an elevated wall, a great profusion of laurel branches were placed upon it, interspered with daffodils, Chinese roses, and marsh marigolds. Over the spring was a square board surrounded with a crown, composed of white and red daisies. The board, being covered with moss, had written upon it in red daisies :

'While He blessed them, He was carried up into Heaven.'

The second well was Hand's Well. This was also

surrounded with laurel branches, and had a canopy
placed over it, covered with polyanthuses. The words
on the canopy were :

> ' The Lord's unsparing hand
> Supplies us with this spring.'

The letters were formed with the bud of the larch,
and between the lines were two rows of purple primroses and marsh marigolds. In the centre above the
spring, on a moss ground, in letters of white daisies :

> ' Sons of Earth
> The triumph join.'

The second Psalm for the day was read here. The
third was Frith's Well. This was greatly admired, as
it was situated in Mr Frith's garden and the shrubs
around it were numerous. Here were formed two
arches, one within the other. The first had a ground
of wild hyacinths and purple primroses, edged with
white, on which was inscribed, in red daisies :

> ' Ascension.'

The receding arch was covered with various flowers,
and in the centre on a ground of marsh marigolds,
edged with wild hyacinths in red daisies :

> ' Peace be unto you.'

Here was read the third Psalm of the day. The
fourth, or Holland's Well, was thickly surrounded
with branches of white thorn, placed in the earth.
This well springs from a small coppice of firs and
thorn. The form of the erection over it was a circular
arch, and in the centre on a ground of marsh mari-

golds, edged with purple primroses, in red daisies these words :

'In God is all.'

At this well was read the Epistle. The fifth, or Goodwin's Well, was surrounded with branches of evergreens, having on a Gothic arch in red daisies :

'He did no sin.'

At this well was read the Gospel. The day concluded by the visitors partaking of the hospitality of the inhabitants, and being gratified with a well-arranged band playing appropriate pieces of music at each other's houses."

This rather lengthy description is worth reproduction, because it shows how an old superstition can be purified of its worst elements, and transformed into a truly Christian celebration. It is noteworthy also as a long-continued and successful protest against the condemnation of such festivals by Bishops and Councils. In itself the festival was as logical, and infinitely more beautiful than, a modern harvest thanksgiving service.

Decorating with rags is a variation difficult to account for. Grose makes an attempt to explain the custom, quoting from an old M.S. :—" Between the towns of Alten and Newton, near the foot of the Rosberrye Toppinge, there is a well dedicated to St. Oswald. The neighbours have an opinion that a shirt, or shift, taken off a sick person and thrown into that well, will show whether the person will recover or die ; for, if it floated, it denoted the recovery of the party ; if it sunk, there remained no hope of their life ; and to reward the saint for his intelligence, they *tear off a rag of the shirt, and leave it hanging on the briers thereabouts;* where," says the writer, " I have seen such numbers as might have made a fayre rheme in a paper-myll."

There is an echo of this theory in *The Statistical Account of Scotland*:—" A spring in the Moss of Melshach, of the chalybeate kind, is still in reputation among the common people. Its sanative qualities extend even to brutes. As this Spring probably obtained vogue at first in days of ignorance and superstition, it would appear that it became customary to leave at the well *part of the clothes of the sick and diseased,* and harness of the cattle, as an offering of gratitude to the divinity who bestowed healing virtues on its waters. And now, even though the superstitious principle no longer exists, the accustomed offerings are still presented."

Again, the same authority says of the parish of Mary-Kirk, Kincardine:—" There is at Balmano a fine spring well, called St. John's Well, which in ancient times was held in great estimation. Numbers who thought its waters of a sanative quality, brought their rickety children to be washed in its stream. Its water was likewise thought a sovereign remedy for sore eyes, which, by frequent washing, was supposed to cure them. To show their gratitude to the saint, and that he might be propitious to continue the virtues of the waters, they put into the well presents, not indeed of any great value, or such as would have been of the least service to him if he had stood in need of money, but such as they conceived the good and merciful apostle, who did not delight in costly oblations, could not fail to accept. The presents generally given were pins, needles, and rags taken from their clothes. This may point out the superstition of those times."

Macaulay in his *History of St. Kilda*, speaking of a consecrated well in that island called Tobirnimbuadh, or the spring of diverse virtues, says that "near the fountain stood an altar, on which the distressed votaries laid down their oblations. Before they could touch sacred water with any prospect of success, it was their constant practice to address the Genius of the place with supplication and prayers. No one approached him with empty hands. But the devotees were abundantly frugal. The offerings presented by them were the poorest acknowledgments that could be made to a superior being, from whom they had either hopes or fears. Shells and pebbles, *rags of linen or stuffs worn out*, pins, needles, or rusty nails, were generally all the tribute that was paid ; and sometimes, though rarely enough, copper coins of the smallest value. Among the heathens of Italy and other countries, every choice fountain was consecrated, and sacrifices were offered to them, as well as to the deities that presided over them. See Ovid's *Fasti*, lib. iii. 300.

'Fonti rex Numa mactat ovem.'

" Horace, in one of his odes, made a solemn promise that he would make a present of a very fine kid, some sweet wine and flowers to a noble fountain in his own Sabine Villa." There appears to be good reason for supporting this theory that the rags and pieces of cloth represent the healing power of the well, a theory which finds confirmation from travellers in other parts

of the world.   Hannay in his *Travels in Persia* says :
" After ten days' journey we arrived at a desolate
caravanserai, where we found nothing but water.   I
observed a tree with a number of rags tied to the
branches : these were so many charms, which
passengers coming from Ghilan, a province remarkable
for agues, had left there, in a fond expectation
of leaving their disease also on the same spot."

Park in his *Travels in the interior of Africa* says :
—" The company advanced as far as a large tree,
called by the natives Neema Taba.   It had a very
singular appearance, being *covered with innumerable
rags or scraps of cloth*, which persons travelling across
the wilderness had at different times tied to its
branches ; a custom so generally followed that no one
passes it without hanging up something."   Mr Park
followed the example, and suspended a handsome
piece of cloth on one of the boughs.

But apart from medical powers, wells were regarded
as possessing occult powers : this is seen in the
existence of the wishing well.   Pennant, in describing
St. Winefred's, says that " near the steps, two feet
beneath the water is a large stone, called the wishing
stone.   It receives many a kiss from the faithful, who
are supposed never to fail in experiencing the com-
pletion of their desires, provided the wish is delivered
with full devotion and confidence."   And Moore in
his *Monastic Remains*, says of Walsingham Chapel,
Norfolk :—" The wishing wells still remain — two
circular stone pits filled with water, enclosed with a
square wall, where the pilgrims used to kneel and
throw in a piece of gold whilst they prayed for the
accomplishment of their wishes."

Reviewing the whole subject, one can see how natural is both the superstition and its gradual disappearance. Not that it has yet disappeared, for large pilgrimages leave this country every year for Lourdes ; and as already stated, St. Winefred's has its yearly visitants. These people would not call themselves superstitious : they believe God and the Virgin are associated with these waters in a special sense, over and above any medical properties such waters may possess, like those of Harrogate, Matlock, and Homburg. The evidence for a divine association is the vision of the Virgin seen by some of the faithful, and when this vision is supported by numerous cures, nothing is wanting to complete conviction. Somebody asks, " Are the cures genuine ? " The answer is, " Many of them are." The true explanation is the effect of mind on body by means of faith. Scores of testimonies outside the Church altogether are to be found in the pages of medical literature, indeed medical men are themselves becoming more and more disinclined to administer drugs, using mental, natural, and dietetic measures instead.[1] But the feelings of the faithful in believing that the Deity has a partiality for wells and fountains is the survival of an ancient superstition, perhaps one might say the most ancient superstition in the world. Everything had its spirit, in the belief of primeval man ; the tree, the brook, the mountain, the cave—each was presided over by a spirit who needed to be propitiated by sacrifice, prayer, or charm, ere the poor human could receive the benefits he sought for. It is a far cry from Animism to Lourdes, but there is a definite con-

[1] See Dr Schofield's *Force of Mind*.

nection between the two.   Both believed in the spirit
of the well.

(2) THE HORN DANCE—ABBOTS BROMLEY.

Mr MacDonagh, in his notes to Sir Benjamin
Stone's *Pictures of National Life and History*, says that
when Henry III. granted the " Charta de Foresta "
there was great rejoicing in some parts of England, and
that the modern horn dance is the repetition of an old
custom instituted to celebrate that event.   " Previous
monarchs had afforested such vast areas that the
greater part of the country had become forest, and
this circumstance, coupled with the very severe
penalties imposed for offences connected with the
chase, had bred much discontent among the people.
The charter restored to them large tracts of land as
well as mitigated the barbarous punishments, mutila-
tion and death being forbidden ; consequently it was
hailed with joy and celebrated with a dramatic form
of dance which was performed in the characters of
stags and huntsmen."

The characters of the dance are curiously dressed
in spotted breeches, and carry reindeer horns
mounted on a pole.   A musician plays an accordion
(which seems an infinite pity) but all the other
implements are kept by the vicar in the church tower.
The early history of the horns is unknown.   There
is a "fool," and Robin Hood and a sportsman make
up the list.   The dance itself is of the nature of a
hunt down the main street.   The " deer " rush away and
the hunters " shoot " them.   The idea is apparently to
assert the rights of the chase.

The use of horns in this case is quite logical and

natural, but there is some obscurity in their use at the Charlton Horn Fair described by Grose. " It consists of a riotous mob, who, after a printed summons dispersed through the adjacent towns, meet at Cuckold's Point, near Deptford, and march from thence in procession through that town and Greenwich to Charlton, with horns of different kinds on their heads ; and at the fair there are sold ram's horns, and every sort of toy made of horn ; even the gingerbread figures have horns." It appears from Fuller's *Whole Life* (1703) that it was the fashion in his time to go to Horn Fair dressed in women's clothes. " I remember being there upon Horn Fair Day, *I was dressed in my landlady's best gown and other women's attire*, and to Horn Fair we went, and as we were coming back by water, all the cloaths were spoiled by dirty water, &c., that was flung on us in an inundation, for which I was obliged to present her with two guineas to make atonement for the damage sustained, &c."

The horns on a stick figure in another custom mentioned by Grose in his *Classical Dictionary of the Mother Tongue* :—

"HIGHGATE. Sworn at Highgate.—A ridiculous custom formerly prevailed at the public houses in Highgate, to administer a ludicrous oath to all travellers of the middling rank who stopped there. The party was sworn on a pair of horns, fastened on a stick ; the substance of the oath was, never to kiss the maid when he could kiss the mistress, never to drink small beer when he could get strong ; with many other injunctions of the like kind, to all which was added the saving clause, ' Unless you like it best.' The person administering the oath was always to be called Father

by the Juror, and he in return was to style him Son,
under the penalty of a bottle."

The ancient use of horns has not yet been solved to
the satisfaction of antiquarians, but at any rate the
Abbot's Bromley ceremony is able to account for
itself in a manner that older and extinct customs
cannot equal.

(3) "TELLING THE BEES."

"A Bedfordshire woman was telling me the other
day," says a writer in a Northern daily paper, "how
her son had been stung all over by bees. 'And no
wonder,' she said, 'he never told them he was going
to put them in a new 'ome, and everybody knows that
before you goes to put bees in a new 'ome, you must
knock three times on the top of the 'ive and tell 'em,
same as you must tell 'em when anyone dies in the
'ouse. Ef you don't, they'll be spiteful, for bees is
understanding creatures, an' knows what you say to
them."

Yes, in secluded villages, among old people, the
bee superstition still exists, but the modern apiarist
will have none of it. To him it is a bit of poetry
from out of the past. And it has some poetry in it;
in fact it is one of the most picturesque of all rural
superstitions, and some of them are neither picturesque
nor decent. Whittier's "Telling the Bees" is so good
a description of the idea that it is worth quoting in
part :—

> "Just the same as a month before,—
> The house and the trees,
> The barn's brown gable, the vine by the door,—
> Nothing changed but the hives of bees.

Before them, under the garden wall,
    Forward and back,
Went drearily singing the chore-girl small,
    Draping each hive with a shred of black.

Trembling, I listened : The summer sun
    Had the chill of snow ;
For I knew she was telling the bees of one
    Gone on the journey we all must go !

Then I said to myself, ' My Mary weeps
    For the dead to-day ;
Haply her blind old grandsire sleeps
    The fret and the pain of his age away.'

But her dog whined low ; on the doorway sill,
    With his cane to his chin,
The old man sat ; and the chore-girl still
    Sung to the bees stealing out and in.

And the song she was singing ever since
    In my ear sounds on :
' Stay at home, pretty bees, fly not hence !
    Mistress Mary is dead and gone ! ' "

Brand does not mention " telling the bees," nor
does Sir Henry Ellis, but the latter has some notes
which apparently go further back than the origin
of the " telling."   In Molle's *Living Libraries* (1621)
we read :—" Who would beleeve without superstition
(if experience did not make it credible), that most
commonly all the bees *die in their hives, if the
master or mistresse of the house chance to die, except the
hives be presently removed into some other place?*
And yet I know this hath hapned to folke no way
stained with superstition."

Here the bees are not to be told of a death in
the house : they die themselves if the hives are not
removed.   In a later century they do not die, but the
hives must be turned round.

I found the following in the "Argus," a London newspaper, Sept. 13, 1790; "A superstitious custom prevails at every funeral in Devonshire, of turning round the bee-hives that belonged to the deceased, if he had any, and that at the moment the corpse is carrying out of the house. At a funeral some time since, at Collumpton, of a rich old farmer, a laughable circumstance of this sort occurred: for, just as the corpse was placed in the hearse, and the horsemen, to a large number, were drawn up in order for the procession of the funeral, a person called out, 'Turn the bees,' when a servant who had no knowledge of such a custom, instead of turning the hives about, lifted them up, and then laid them down on their sides. The bees, thus hastily invaded, instantly attacked and fastened on the horses and their riders. It was in vain they galloped off, the bees as precipitately followed, and left their stings as marks of their indignation. A general confusion took place, attended with loss of hats, wigs, etc., and the corpse during the conflict was left unattended; nor was it till after a considerable time that the funeral attendants could be rallied, in order to proceed to the interment of their deceased friend."

If one must find a suitable source for all these varying ideas about bees and bee hives, it can only be in the mysteries surrounding the activities and habits of bees, now much better understood than they used to be; and in the manner in which signs of a religious nature were sought and found in daily phenomena. To the intelligence of the peasant a bee could not but provide marvels sufficient to win his respect, if not something more; for the bee worked industriously and cleverly on behalf of the peasant, and asked no wages. In other words, the peasant was a debtor to the bee, and his attitude was one of gratitude. Out of this feeling, no doubt, arose a sense of identity in interests—a fellow-feeling which prompted him to "tell the bees" of a death, and to turn the hive at a burial.

The religious element is seen in a letter, dated 1811, contributed to *The Gentleman's Magazine*. The writer says : " There is in this part of Yorkshire a custom which has been by the country-people more or less revived, ever since the alteration in the style and calendar : namely, the watching in the midnight of the new and old 'Xmas Eve by bee-hives, to determine upon the right 'Xmas from the humming noise which they suppose the bees will make when the birth of our Saviour took place. Disliking innovations, the utility of which they understand not, the oracle, they affirm, always prefers the most antient custom." This is a good instance of using bees as a means of divination, and when once a people start divining, a crowd of omens is sure to follow in their train.

The theory that when the bees in a farmer's hives die, he will soon be compelled to move from the farm, is easily accounted for by Mr Gibson. " A hive of bees rarely dies unless the season is so bad that it is disastrous to farming ; consequently, where a farmer holds his farm on a yearly tenancy, it may follow that he will find it necessary to go elsewhere to build up his fortune." [1]

---

[1] *Superstitions about Animals*, p. 168.

(4) The Death-Bell.

Once called the passing-bell, or the soul-bell,
the death-bell is still a modern fact in some parts
of the country, being rung, according, to rules,
on the death of a parishioner; there are knells for
men, for women, and for children. Of course, bells
are as old as creation—in China they date back
to times beyond the Bible record. The point we
have to settle is: why did the clergy ring the bell
when a member of the congregation died?   The first
answer is: he rung it, or caused it to be rung, *before*
the member died; that is, whilst praying for the
dead and ringing for the dead were practically
identical, there was a preliminary ringing before death
took place.

The following clause, in the " Advertisements for
due Order, etc.," in the 7th year of Queen Elizabeth,
is much to our purpose :—

" Item, that when anye Christian bodie is *in passing*,
that *the bell be tolled*, and that the curate be speciallie
called for to comforte the sicke person ; and *after the
time of his passinge*, to ringe no more but one short
peale ; and one before the buriall, and another short
peale after the buriall."

But the ringing is not explained in this ancient
order; it does no more than give the ecclesiastical
rule. Grose goes deeper into the subject. " The
passing-bell," he says, " was anciently rung for two
purposes : one, to bespeak the prayers of all good
Christians for a soul just departing; the other, to
drive away the evil spirits who stood at the bed's
foot and about the house, ready to seize their prey,

or at least to molest and terrify the soul in its passage: but by the ringing of that bell (for Durandus informs us evil spirits are much afraid of bells) they were kept aloof; and the soul, like a hunted hare, gained the start, or had what is by sportsmen called law."

" Hence, perhaps, exclusive of the additional labour, was occasioned the high price demanded for tolling the greatest bell of the church; for, that being louder, the evil spirits must go farther off to be clear of its sound, by which the poor soul got so much more the start of them: besides, being heard farther off, it would likewise procure the dying man a greater number of prayers. This dislike ot spirits to bells is mentioned in the Golden Legend by Wynkyn de Worde."

I fear we shall have to admit the accuracy of this statement about driving away the devils. Naturally we have long since discarded the superstition; and to-day the tolling is soft and subdued; but, as the question of origins is the one uppermost in this book, we have no option but to confess that the underlying idea was two-fold: to call the living Christian to prayer, and to scare the fiends who were waiting to pounce on a departing soul.

(5) VAMPIRES.

To find the first references to vampires, we have to go back to the records of Chaldea and Assyria, but these records do no more than inform us of a current belief in the existence and raids of these monsters; there is nothing to explain their origin and nothing to justify them. They are accepted as facts. In some quarters of the globe, especially on the European Continent, Servia, Austria, and parts of the Balkans, the dread of the vampire is still a living force; not with people of intelligence and education, but with the uninstructed peasantry. And yet it would not be fair to the countries named to generalise so freely, and a strict regard for truth compels us to say that the vampire superstition lives in those isolated districts where the tradition of its ravages is strongest.

Mr Bram Stoker's *Dracula* aroused a good deal of interest in this country as to the reality of phenomena recorded in history ; and when it was followed by " Modern Vampirism : its dangers and how to avoid them," by A. O. Eaves, a book on which I shall have something to say later, it is clear that there yet lingers among us a kind of half notion that Vampirism may contain a germ of truth.

That Vampirism is not an exploded superstition is evident from an even earlier book, which bears the name of Herbert Mayo, M.D., formerly Senior Surgeon of Middlesex Hospital, and Professor of Anatomy and Physiology at King's College. The book is intitled, *On the Truths contained in Popular Superstitions*, and is dated 1851. After describing the alleged methods of vampires and the means of avoiding their attacks (according to the best authorities), Dr. Mayo goes on to say, " This is no romancer's dream. It is a succinct account of a superstition which to this day survives in the East of Europe, where little more than a century ago it was frightfully prevalent. At that period Vampirism

spread like a pestilence through Servia and
Wallachia, causing numerous deaths, and disturbing
all the land with fear of the mysterious visitation
against which none felt himself secure. Here is something like a good, solid, practical, popular delusion. Do
I believe it? To be sure I do. The facts are matters
of history ; the people died like rotted sheep ;
and the cause and method of their dying was, in
their belief, what has just been stated." Dr. Mayo
then begins to establish the reasons why he believed
the phenomena of Vampirism were real in the places
mentioned, quoting at length the evidence of a
document signed by three regimental surgeons, and
formally countersigned by a lieutenant - colonel
and sub-lieutenant. The date is June 7, 1732, and
the place is Mednegna, near Belgrade. A specimen
case will give the reader an idea of its contents.
" A woman of the name of Miliza had died at the
end of a three months' illness. The body had been
buried ninety odd days. In the chest was liquid
blood. The body was declared by a heyduk, who
recognised it, to be in better condition and fatter
than it had been in the woman's life-time." This
is in keeping with the theory that a vampire is
"a dead body which continues to live in the grave ;
which it leaves, however, by night, for the purpose
of sucking the blood of the living, whereby it is
nourished and preserved in good condition."
Dealing with the physiology of the matter first
of all, Dr Mayo contends that an epidemic of
Vampirism may be started by a few premature burials ;
and that they are the bodies of persons who have been
buried alive. This statement is quite sufficiently

startling to compel a pause. A lot of people are buried before they are dead, if we are to believe in the testimony of careful inquirers, and yet we do not seem to have outbreaks of Vampirism as they had in the eighteenth century. Besides, what has become of the possibility of smothering a man to death by screwing him down in a coffin, and interring him in seven feet of earth ? What is there after that to keep the average stockbroker from resuming life and activity ? These are questions which cannot be set aside.

Dr Mayo can find no satisfactory explanation of the activity of the vampire when on the rampage. It is the *ghost* of the vampire which visits the victim and sucks his blood : a very substantial ghost, indeed. But he thinks the death-trance of the victim may become epidemic, acting by means of suggestion. Very true ; the whole thing is suggestion from beginning to end. We have only to make people believe in the possibility of being operated upon after the manner of the vampire, and imagination will do the rest.

It is distinctly annoying to take up a modern book on the subject and find that the author's first words are : " Want of space will prevent elaborate and detailed proofs being given of the statements made in the following paper. Most of the statements made have been verified by more than one of the investigators into the subjects dealt with, observers who have developed within themselves extensions of faculties possessed by all, but latent as yet in most of us[1]." When Mr A. O. Eaves starts out

[1] *Modern Vampirism: Its dangers and how to avoid them.*

in this manner, we know what value to place upon
his stories, his arguments, and his conclusions. Of
course, to him the origin of vampire superstitions
is in the fact that vampires have always existed.
A bad man dies and can't get away from his earth
life. He strives to come back again into earthly
conditions, and Vampirism is one of the ways open
to him. Says Mr Eaves :—" In the case of those
removed by accident, or suicide, in which no
preparation of any kind has been made, and where
all the life-forces are in full play, if the life has
been a degraded one, then they will be alive to
the horrors of this plane. They will be cut adrift,
as it were, with all their passional nature strong
upon them, and must remain on that plane until
the time their death in an ordinary manner would
have taken place. Thus a man killed at 25, who
would otherwise have reached the age of 75, would
spend half a century upon this plane. In case of
the suicides, seeing they have not accomplished
their end, viz., to put an end to existence, the
return for earth-life grows upon them with terrible
zest."

" It is here that one of the dangers of Vampirism
occurs. If the experience they seek cannot be
obtained without a physical body, only two courses
are open for them. One is to do so vicariously. To
do this, they must feed on the emanations arising
from blood and alcohol ; public houses and slaughter-
houses are thronged with these unhappy creatures,
which hang about and feed thus. From this standpoint the habit of offering blood-sacrifices to
propitiate entities, as found recorded in some of

the world-scriptures, becomes luminous, and the history of magic teems with such examples. Not content, however, with thus prolonging their existence on the lower level of the astral plane, the entities lure on those human beings whose tastes are depraved, causing them to go to all kinds of excesses, enticing them on in sensuality and vice of every kind. Each time a man yields to temptation, the supremacy over him which these creatures hold becomes the stronger ; they gain possession of his will, till at length they control him altogether. How many men, who have hitherto lived a blameless life, have on the spur of the moment committed some heinous crime, and the public have marvelled how they came to do it. The explanation offered after the commission of the crime has often been to the effect that they could not tell what possessed them to do it, but they felt a sudden impulse sweep over them and they obeyed it. Here, without doubt, is the genesis of the conception of a tempter, and one feels more inclined to pity than to blame in many cases."

If the censorship of books is needed, it is needed in such cases as *Modern Vampirism*. A young girl of highly nervous temperament might easily be obsessed by reading it, purely through the action of imagination. Mr Eaves is quite sincere, and means well, but the mischief of his book in some hands is palpable. No doubt, to think and live purely is, as he says, a "defence" ; it is a defence against many evils on the ordinary plane of life ; but when he advocates a plentiful use of garlic and the placing of small saucers of nitric acid to scare away vampires, we wonder whether we are still in the middle ages.

To recapitulate : The origin of vampire superstitions must be sought in the ignorance of early races who buried their dead in the earth, for it is singular that the races which cremate their dead have been practically free from vampire legends. Earth burial has never been free from the possibility of premature interment, and although there is no reason to believe that a man buried alive will not die in his coffin of suffocation, an ignorant peasantry seemed to imagine that he could live, issue forth at night, and keep himself alive by sucking the blood of the living. It is notable that as disbelief in this notion assumed large proportions, owing to the advance of education and refinement, the phenomena disappeared. Visitations as recorded in history have borne the marks of an epidemic, and even Dr Mayo was not averse to the proposition that a man who had a wasting disease, or was threatened with one, could imagine himself vampirised and thus spread the contagion to others. Vampirism is only another proof of the power of the mind over the body. It is the *fixed idea* that does the work. Mr Stanley Redgrove quotes an illustration from J. G. Fraser's *Psyche's Task* :—

" In illustration of the real power of the imagination, we may instance the Maori superstition of the Taboo. According to the Maoris, any one who touches a tabooed object will assuredly die, the tabooed object being a sort of ' anti-talisman.' Professor Frazer says :—' Cases have been known of Maoris dying of sheer fright on learning that they had unwittingly eaten the remains of a chief's dinner, or handled something that belonged to him,' since such objects were *ipso facto* tabooed. He gives the following case

on good authority : ' A woman, having partaken of
some fine peaches from a basket, was told that they
had come from a tabooed place. Immediately the
basket dropped from her hands and she cried out in
agony that the *atua* or godhead of the chief, whose
divinity had been thus profaned, would kill her.
That happened in the afternoon, and next day by
twelve o'clock she was dead.' For us the power of
the taboo does not exist ; for the Maori, who implicitly
believes in it, it is a very potent reality, but this
power of the taboo resides, not in the external objects,
but in his own mind." Very true. And the power
of the vampire is the power of the idea.

(6) ROBIN REDBREAST.

Birds have always figured conspicuously in pagan
superstitions, and it is possible that the superstitions
which still linger among us, in some places at least,
with regard to certain English birds, may be an echo
of the older variety. Robins are held in high esteem
by most people, except gardeners and farmers, an
esteem which is partly accounted for by their coloured
breasts and partly by the song-powers of the male
bird. Probably, too, this esteem arises out of the old
time superstition referred to in ancient ballads,
beginning with " The Babes in the Wood." Percy
says :—

> " No burial this pretty pair
> Of any man receives,
> Till Robin Redbreast painfully,
> Did cover them with leaves."

From this fancy seems to have grown the notion
that it is unlucky to kill or keep a robin, and this is

alluded to in the following lines of an eighteenth
century poet, which occur in an ode to the Robin :

> " For ever from his threshold fly,
> Who, void of honour, once shall try,
> With base inhospitable breast,
> To bar the freedom of his guest ;
> O rather seek the peasant's shed,
> For he will give thee wasted bread,
> And fear some new calamity,
> Should any there spread snares for thee."
> J. H. Pott's Poems, 1780.

Whatever fancy and superstition may do by way of
investing the robin with a glory that does not belong
to him, the plain truth is that there is no more
impertinent or mischievous thief in the whole tribe of
feathers.

(7) DRINKING CUSTOMS: TOASTS.

When John Smith raises his glass in the saloon
bar of " The World's End," and proposes the health
of his friend, John Jones, he little thinks he is per-
petuating a custom which goes back in unbroken
succession to the days of the Greeks and Romans.
A Roman gallant would drink as many glasses as
there were letters in the name of his mistress.
Thus Martial :—

> " Six cups to Naevia's health go quickly round,
> And he with seven the fair Justina crowned."

The Tatler (vol. i. 24) ventures to account for the
origin of the word toast in the following manner,
stating that it had its rise from an accident at Bath
in the reign of Charles the Second :—" It happened
that, on a public day, a celebrated beauty of those
times was in the Cross Bath, and one of the crowd

of her admirers took a glass of the water in which the fair one stood, and drank her health to the company. There was in the place a gay fellow, half fuddled, who offered to jump in, and swore, though he liked not the liquor, he would have the toast. He was opposed in his resolution; yet this whim gave foundation to the present honour which is done to the lady we mention in our liquor, who has ever since been called a toast." This is not convincing, although it cannot be disproved. But in a book called *Checmonopagerion*, by R. Thorius (1651), the following passages occur :—

> " Cast wood upon the fire, thy loyns gird round
> With warmer clothes, and let the *tosts* abound
> *In close array, embattel'd on the hearth.*"

So again :—

> " And tell their hard adventures by the fire,
> While their friends hear, and hear, and more desire,
> And all the time the crackling chesnuts roast,
> And *each man hath his cup*, and *each his toast.*"

From these passages it is apparent that the saying, " *Who gives a toast?* " is synonymous with " Whose turn is it to take up his cup and propose a health? " It was the practice to put *toast into ale with nutmeg and sugar.* Evidently the "toast" as we know it to-day began in this practice, and a good "toaster" was described with accuracy so far back as 1684 in *The New Help to Discourse.*

> " TOAST,
> Anagram
> A SOTT.
> Exposition.

"A Toast is like a Sot ; or, what is most
Comparative, a Sot is like a Toast ;
For when their substances in liquor sink,
Both properly are said to be in drink."

(8) YEW TREES IN CHURCHYARDS.

There are many theories to account for the ancient
practice of planting churchyards and cemeteries with
yew trees.   Some authorities ascribe it to the adoption of ancient funeral rites ; others to the prosaic
notion of keeping the wind off the church ; others,
again, to the warlike need of bows and arrows—yew
being especially serviceable.   A large body of writers
believe the use of the yew was symbolic—it typified
by its unchanging verdure the doctrine of the resurrection.   A few cynically assert that yews, being
gloomy and poisonous, are rightly used for churchyard decoration ; and there are not wanting writers
who see in the practice a tribute to the superstitious
regard men have always paid to trees.   We may
examine one or two of these suggestions, although
no definite conclusion may be possible.   We know
that the ancient Britons planted yews near their
temples long before Christianity was introduced
into England, and this would suggest a custom on
the island not necessarily Roman or Christian.[1]   A
writer in *The Gentleman's Magazine* (1781) says :—

"We read in the Antiquities of Greece and Rome
that the branches of the cypress and yew were the

---

[1] "The yew was a funereal tree, the companion of the grave, among
the Celtic tribes.   'Here,' says the bard, speaking of the two departed
lovers, 'rests their dust, Cuthullin !   These lonely yews sprang from
heir tomb, and shade them from the storm !'"   Ossian, vol. i. p. 240.

usual signals to denote a house in mourning. Now,
sir, as Death was a deity among the antients (the
daughter of Sleep and Night), and was by them
represented in the same manner, with the addition
only of a long robe embroidered with stars, I think
we may fairly conclude that the custom of planting
the yew in churchyards took its rise from Pagan
superstition, and that it is as old as the conquest
of Britain by Julius Cæsar."

Gough, in the Introduction to his second volume
of *Sepulchral Monuments in Great Britain,* speaking
of the signs of death in houses among the ancients,
notices branches of *pine* and *cypress,* on the authority
of Euripides, Hecuba, 191, 192 ; Suet. Aug. 101 ;
Æn. xi. 31. He says in a note, " Will it be thought
a far-fetcht conjecture that yew-trees in churchyards
supply the place of cypress round tombs, where Ovid,
Trist. III. xiii. 21, says they were placed ? "

Far-fetched or not, the evidence is too slight to
enable us to say confidently that the use of the yew
comes to us from Pagan times.

Barrington, in his *Observations on the Statutes,* says
"that trees in a churchyard were often planted to
skreen the church from the wind ; that, low as churches
were built at this time, the thick foliage of the yew
answered this purpose better than any other tree.
I have been informed, accordingly, that the yew-
trees in the churchyard of Gyffin, near Conway,
having been lately felled, the roof of the church
hath suffered excessively."

This sounds like a purely private opinion, and may
be dismissed without further argument. There is a
good deal to be said for the growing of yews to

make bows. Sir Henry Ellis remarks that Shakespeare in *Richard II.* speaks of *the double fatal yew*
because the leaves of the yew are poison, and the
wood is employed for instruments of death. On
this Stevens observes, that "from some of the ancient
statutes it appears that every Englishman, while
archery was practised, was obliged to keep in his
house either a bow of yew or some other wood. It
should seem, therefore, that yews were not only
planted in churchyards to defend the churches from
the wind, but on account of their use in making bows ;
while by the benefit of being secured in inclosed
places, their poisonous quality was kept from doing
mischief to cattle."

The difficulty of this otherwise reasonable conjecture is seen in the question : Are not all plantation
grounds fenced from cattle ? And why are there no
more than two yew trees in each churchyard if bow
wood was so necessary ?

Sir Thomas Browne, in his *Hydriotaphia Urne-
buriall*, tell us, that among the ancients, "the funerall
pyre consisted of sweet fuell, cypresse, firre, larix,
YEWE, and trees perpetually verdant." And he asks,
or rather observes, "Whether the planting of *yewe*
in churchyards holds its original from ancient funerall
rites, or as an embleme of resurrection from its
perpetual verdure, may also admit conjecture."

Yes, it admits of conjecture, and in all likelihood
man's choice of the yew for funeral associations was
determined by its appearance, its longevity, its utility
in supplying material for weapons, and its need of
segregation on account of its poisonous qualities ; in
fact, nearly all the suggested facts seem to have

played some part in establishing the yew tree where
we mostly find it.

(9) THEATRE SUPERSTITIONS.

It is curious that Brand should not have noticed
the superstitions of actors and actresses, for they are
as essentially a modern growth as those he has dealt
with so fully were of ancient origin ; moreover, to
compare the two together is to see striking points of
difference and analogy.   The difference is that the
superstitions of the theatre are all of them based on a
firm belief in the principle of Luck ; they are secular
from beginning to end, and without a spark of religious association.   The analogy lies in the fact that,
like many of the old superstitions, they are ground-
less for the most part, being no more than *ipse dixits*
of leading artists, supposed to be borne out by the
experience of the rank and file.

To whistle in a theatre is a sign of the worst
luck in the world, and there is no offence for which
the manager will scold an employee more quickly.
Vaudeville performers believe it is bad luck to change
the costumes in which they first achieved success.
Old actors believe the witches' song in *Macbeth* to
possess the uncanny power of casting evil spells,
and the majority of them strongly dislike to play in
the piece.   Hum the tune in the hearing of an old
actor and the chances are you will lose his friendship.
Actors will not repeat the last lines of a play at re-
hearsals, nor will they go on the stage where there is
a picture of an ostrich if they can avoid it.   Let them
try the handle of a wrong door when seeking the

manager of a theatre, or the office of an agent, and they regard it as an omen of failure. The looping of a drop curtain, the upsetting of a make-up box, are the certain forerunners of evil, just as certain shades of yellow in a tie, or vest, or hat, are thought to exert an injurious influence. Even the orchestra leader would not allow a musician to play a yellow clarionet —everything would go wrong if he did. Faults of memory are also attributed by actors to the costume he may be wearing. Certain wigs bring luck, and some actors will wear one even though the part does not need one.

" If an actor's shoes squeak while he is making his first entrance, it is a sure sign that he will be well received by the audience.

" To kick off his shoes and have them alight on their soles and remain standing upright, means good luck to him, but if they fall over, bad luck is to be expected. They will also bring him all kinds of misfortune if placed on a chair in the dressing-room.

" If, when an acrobat throws his cuffs on the stage, preparatory to doing his turn, they remain fastened together, all will go well; but if, on the other hand, they separate, he must look out for squalls.

" Cats have always been considered the very best fortune-producing acquisitions a theatre can possess, and are welcomed and protected by actor and stage-hand alike. But if a cat runs across the stage during the action of the play, misfortune is sure to follow. Bad luck will also come to those who kick a cat.

" The actor goes the layman one better in mirror

superstitions. He believes it will bring him bad luck to have another person look into the mirror over his shoulder while he is making up before it.

" As much care must be taken by the actor on making his entrances as in the repeating of the lines. Not for their importance as an effect on the audience, but to avoid the ' hoodoo ' attached to certain entries. For example : To stumble over anything on making an entrance, the actor firmly believes, will cause him to miss a cue or forget his lines.

" If his costume catches on a piece of scenery as he goes on, he must immediately retrace his steps and make a new entrance, or else suffer misfortunes of all sorts during the rest of the performance.

" Even the drop-curtain contributes its share of stage superstitions, as nearly every actor and manager believes it is bad luck to look out at the audience from the wrong side of it when it is down. Some say it is the prompt side that casts the evil spell, while others contend it is the opposite side. The management not being sure from which side the bad luck is likely to accrue, places a peep-hole directly in the centre.

" The players are not the only ones in the theatre having superstitions. The ' front of the house ' have their pet ones as well.

" In the box-office, if the first purchaser of seats for a new production is an old man or woman, it means to the ticket-seller that the play will have a long run. A young person means the reverse. A torn bank-note means a change of position for the man in the box-office, while a gold certificate, strange to say, is a sign of bad luck.

" The usher seating the first patron of the evening
fondly imagines that he will be lucky until the end of
the performance, but if the first coupon he handles
calls for one of the many thirteen seats, he is quite
sure that it will bring him bad luck for the rest of the
night."

To the usher, a tip from a woman for a programme
also spells misfortune, and few of the old-timers will
accept it.   A woman fainting in the theatre is sure to
bring bad luck to the usher in whose section she is
seated.   Not to hear the first lines of the play is to
invite misfortune, so he believes.

" An usher feels sure that if he makes a mistake in
seating the first person in his section, it is sure to be
quickly followed by two more.   The first tip of the
season is always briskly rubbed on the trousers-leg,
and kept in the pocket for the rest of the season as a
'coaxer.'   To receive a smile over the footlights from
one of the company also brings luck." [1]

It would be a futile task to try to discover the
origin of all these separate superstitions.   Fortunately
it is not necessary, for there is an easier and more
natural solution.   The omens and mascots of stage
life have their source in the artistic temperament.   We
do not find these superstitions in the life of the music
hall artist, at least not in the same degree ; and whilst
the actor-manager of a theatre might have some
scruples for the superstitions of the profession, the
manager of a music hall would have none at all,
because he faces business on a purely business basis.
Now, that is the difference between the actor-man

[1] For the details in this section I am indebted to an entertaining
article in *The Scrap Book*.

and the commercial-man ; the former has to deal with a crowd of uncertainties—the fickleness of the public, the machinery of the stage, the health of the troupe, lapses of memory, and a score of other items equally trying. Add to this the constant endeavour to *act* a picture in his own mind, or to *interpret* a part in a classic drama, and you have a psychology full of weird possibilities in its conclusions. Viewed from this standpoint, the actor's superstitions are to some extent natural ; were he not of the artistic tempera- ment he would be lacking in the sympathy his art requires. But still, he would not be the worse for shedding a few of these intellectual oddities ; for, after all, most of them are based in fear and a lack of self- confidence.

(10) Christening Ships.

When the wife of some Admiralty official touches a button to release a new cruiser from the stays, and breaks a bottle of wine over her bows, the spectators accept these actions as the right thing, because they have been performed for centuries. But the spectators do not usually enquire into the origin of the custom, to discover which we have to go back to the ancient libations practised on the launching of a new vessel. A priest with a lighted torch, and possessed also of an egg and some brimstone, was in attendance ; and amid shouts of acclamation it was devoted to the god whose image it carried. Greek and Roman vessels generally carried in the prow a carved image of some deity, to whose name the launching service was dedicated. The image remained as a feature of ship-

Q

building until quite recent years, and we retain a semblance of the old ceremony.

(11) HORSESHOE TRIBUTES IN OAKHAM CASTLE.

Evelyn, on August 14, 1654, tells us that he " took a journey in the Northern parts," and in passing through Oakham he saw some of the celebrated shoes on the Castle gates. Mr Michael M'Donagh says : " Perhaps the most singular mediæval tribute now exacted is the horseshoe required from every peer who passes through Oakham. Originally the shoe had to come from the actual horse ridden by a baron ; but for a long time it has been usual to commute the toll by paying for a fancy shoe, and as a result the tributes in Oakham Hall vary greatly in shape and size, and are even made of different metals. They are mostly dated, the most important exception being a large shoe given by Queen Elizabeth, who probably sent it about 1556, after her visit to Lord Burghley. Among them are several from the Royal Family—Queen Victoria (when Princess Victoria) in 1835 ; Queen Alexandra (when Princess of Wales) in 1881 ; and his Majesty the King (when Prince of Wales) in 1895. In all, there are nearly 200 shoes which are of all sizes, from seven feet in length down to one only big enough for the small-hoofed race horse." This tribute has been demanded for seven centuries, and tradition ascribes its origin to the truculent Walchelin de Ferreris, to whom Henry II. gave the Barony of Oakham.

(12) The Duty of Not Saving a Drowning Man.

If ever there existed an inhuman superstition, surely this is the one; for to see a fellow mortal fighting for life, and to refuse to render him assistance, is the height of cruelty. But, the reader will ask, does such a superstition really exist? Tylor speaks of "a recent account (1864)" where fishermen in Bohemia did not venture to snatch a drowning man from the waters, the notion being that some ill luck would follow. Sir Walter Scott in the *Pirate* speaks of Bryce, the pedlar, refusing to save the shipwrecked sailor from drowning, and even remonstrating with him on the rashness of such a deed. "Are you mad?" said the pedlar, "you that have lived sae lang in Zetland to risk the saving of a drowning man? Wot ye not, if you bring him to life again he will be sure to do you some capital injury?" The same superstition can be found among the St. Kilda islanders, the boatmen of the Danube, French and English sailors, and even out of Europe, and among less civilised races. If these statements be correct, and Professor Tylor's name is behind them,[1] what is at the back of this determination to let a drowning man drown? The idea seems to be this: that when a man is drowning it is the intention of the gods that he should be drowned; and that the rescuer, if successful in rescuing him, must be the substitute and be drowned himself later on. You cannot cheat Fate out of a life; that appears to be the argument. Even an accidental falling into the water is explained by

the savage as the action of the spirit throwing the
man into the stream with the object of taking his
life. The indisposition of many people to try to
rescue such may in part be explained by Tylor's
theory of *Survival*, a theory suggesting that the
thoughts and actions of the past are repeated by us
unconsciously. It cannot be that the paragraph in the
Press about the callous conduct of observers is *always*
due to cowardice—the fear to plunge in and effect
a rescue. Nor can it be the conscious inability to do
anything, or the paralysis of mind due to the sight of
a fellow-man on the point of sinking for the last time.
It must be some small remainder of a once prevalent
and all prevailing notion that to attempt to save a
drowning man was unlucky.

(13) PLAYING CARD SUPERSTITIONS.

It is somewhat singular that Brand should have
confined his notes to the growth of the various card
games in England, omitting entirely all reference to
the superstitions which cloud the atmosphere of the
gambler, and even the card player who does not
play for money, or, if he does, for very small stakes.
In games of chance and skill combined, we find
just that sort of uncertain feeling which provokes
all kinds of theories as to what is right and wrong;
the right and wrong in this association meaning
no more than success or failure. A search for such
superstitious theories is speedily rewarded; the joint
authors of *The Encyclopædia of Superstitions* have
collected quite a little crowd of them; some old,
some new; some whimsical and without reason;
others indicative of observation, and having a basis in

common-sense. I propose first to enumerate a few of them, and afterwards to make an attempt at the discovery of their origin.

OMENS RELATING TO CARD GAMES.

1. To play cards on the table without a table-cloth is unlucky.
2. He who lends money at play will lose; he who borrows money at play will win.
3. In playing cards, walk straight from the table and make a round turn, if playing for money.
4. There is a superstition at Monto Carlo that immediately after a suicide all those playing against the bank will win. There is therefore a perfect rush for the tables when the lugubrious news is known.
5. If you wish a person to win at cards, stick a pin in his coat.
6. To drop a card on the floor when playing is a bad omen.
7. To sing while playing cards is a sign that your side will lose.
8. Don't play at a table with a cross-eyed man whether he is your partner or opponent; you will lose.
9. If you get into a passion when playing cards you will have more bad luck; for the demon of bad luck always follows a passionate player.

It is truly difficult to imagine how the first item could have originated; there is absolutely no sense in a connection between skill in a game and the covering of the table on which it is played; if the objection had arisen out of the difference between

a mahogany table and a steel table, one might
have fancied electric forces, or mesmeric forces, had
something to do with the origin of this vain notion.
It has been suggested that the table-cloth gives
an opportunity of "manipulating" cards which a
bare table does not. Perhaps. And yet *all* superstitions cannot have arisen in the minds of cheats and
dubious people.

No. 2 is contrary to experience, at anyrate the
second half is. The plunger who will lose all his own
money and borrows to continue playing, generally
loses.

No. 3 has a touch of humour in it—grim humour,
no doubt. It seems to come from the heart of a wily
but skilful player, who knows the fascination of
the game to the novice with keenly awakened desires ;
and when age and experience speak they counsel
a walk away from the table, "a round turn" and
——— well, that is just it ; it is a chance afforded
the player to *think*. "Shall I play or shall I not
—for it is for money ?" This is about as sensible
a bit of superstition as could be invented.

No. 4 is a specimen of the modern mind at work.
And how like the old mind ! It is as if the
players said, "The God of Chance has had a big
success ; he has won thousands and thousands ;
and he has driven his victim to suicide and death.
He *can't* be the same god for a day or two ; we must
give him time to get over the dreadful event. So we
will play whilst he is sorrowing." This logic would
hardly do credit to a Comanche Indian, but there it is
all the same. A Monto Carlo player commits
suicide, and there follows a rush for the tables.

Why? Because the players believe in luck, and for some reason they fancy a sufferer's death must inevitably turn the tide in favour of themselves.

The crooked pin referred to in No. 5 is an idea borrowed from other sources. Brand has a note to the effect that:—"About a mile to the west of Jarrow (near Newcastle-upon-Tyne) there is a well, still called *Bede's Well*, to which as late as the year 1740 it was a prevailing custom to bring children troubled with any disease or infirmity; a crooked pin was put in, and the well laved dry between each dipping. My informant has seen twenty children brought together on a Sunday to be dipped in this well, at which also, on Midsummer Eve, there was a great resort of neighbouring people, with bonfires, musick, etc."

No. 6 is a bad omen, because it suggests careless handling of the cards on account of lack of interest, and not watching the progress of the game; and No. 7 is even stronger in this respect. No. 9 belongs to the same category, only in this case the player is giving an excited attention to the game, and loses his head. No. 8 is apparently a joke pure and simple.

Every card player has his own or her own private superstitions: a certain hand always presages good luck or ill-luck; the winning of the first game means winning the third; to play before 6 p.m. on Fridays is never fortunate, and so on. But the whole batch of card superstitions has its source in an attempt to formulate laws for the one thing that seems to have no law—chance.

INDEX.